MULTINATIONAL CORPORATIONS AND WORLD ORDER

Edited by

George Modelski

 SAGE PUBLICATIONS *Beverly Hills / London*

PUBLISHER'S NOTE

The material in this publication originally appeared as a special issue of INTER-NATIONAL STUDIES QUARTERLY (Volume 16, Number 4, December 1972). The Publisher would like to acknowledge the assistance of the International Studies Association and the special issue editor, George Modelski, in making this edition possible.

For information address:

SAGE PUBLICATIONS, INC.
275 South Beverly Drive
Beverly Hills, California 90212

SAGE PUBLICATIONS LTD
St George's House / 44 Hatton Garden
London EC1N 8ER

Printed in the United States of America

International Standard Book Number 0-8039-0317-0

Library of Congress Catalog Card No. 73-87854

FIRST PRINTING (this edition)

CONTENTS

Multinational Business

A Global Perspective

GEORGE MODELSKI
Department of Political Science
University of Washington

A source of hope for some and of apprehension for others, multinational business is now recognized as a potentially powerful force for giving shape to world society. The advocates, or even the philosophers, of the multinational corporation have not been wanting in eloquence. They have especially claimed for this new instrumentality—beyond efficiency and productivity—high social merit in the global context (Ball, 1967: 80; Fortune, 1969; Peccei, 1971: 9; Brown, 1970: 7-8). In their enthusiasm and exuberance, they recall nineteenth-century optimism about the simple virtues of international trade as the universal force for peace. But a strong body of thought exists that denies such claims and asserts opposite views. Using arguments first elaborated by J. A. Hobson, an English pacifist writing at the turn of the century, such critics were early to recognize the global operating capacity of the corporate form of organization while rejecting the notion that it had positive effects either for social justice or for world order. Against the background of hostility to 'capitalism,' they invested business enterprises which were operating beyond the frontiers of the

AUTHOR'S NOTE: This is a revised version of a paper presented at the one hundred thirty-ninth meeting of the American Association for the Advancement of Science, Philadelphia, December 1971.

[5]

home society with sinister meaning, seeing the competitive search for overseas markets and raw materials all too easily translated into intergovernmental conflict and, ultimately, war.[1] More recently, they have been revived in some current interpretations of American foreign policy, and the upsurge of specifically multinational business has given them a new lease on life (see Magdoff, 1969).

To answer the critics, we shall review available empirical materials to determine the direct links, if any, between multinational corporations and war and peace. To probe the claims of the advocates, we shall follow this up with a more general discussion of the place of multinational business in schemes for world order. But first, a definition of the nature of multinational business seems in point.

World Distribution of Multinational Business

The line separating multinational from other kinds of business is not easily drawn, Obviously, not *all* business is multinational business. Not even all *big* business is multinational business; some large firms—for instance, in merchandising and distribution—orient themselves solely to one national market. In this article, a firm will be deemed multinational if its principal operating facilities are located in more than a minimal (say two or three) number of countries; operationally, this property may be determined by ascertaining the number of "foreign" branches or subsidiaries associated with a given company.

Worldwide, most multinational business activity now originates either in North America (the United States and Canada), in Western Europe, or in Japan.[2]

1. For a discussion of Marxist perspectives on world business, see von Krosigk's contribution to this issue.
2. The Soviet sphere shows little evidence of multinational economic activity. The "joint" companies organized after 1945 by the USSR in Eastern Europe and the Far East in a number of important industries (including oil and uranium) but largely discontinued after 1956 did not satisfy the criteria of multinationality. Some more recent "joint venture"-type projects (such as pipelines) may be nearer to them.

THE UNITED STATES

In the global picture, United States-based enterprises easily predominate. In the mid-sixties, some sixty percent of the book value of the world's direct (as distinct from portfolio) foreign investments was attributable to American companies (Hellman, 1970: 5). If American overseas investment were considered jointly with Canadian, British, and Dutch corporate activities, the total share of this frequently interlocking system rises to over eighty percent.[3]

American predominance in this field is of quite long standing, because the management and operation of mining and manufacturing establishments in foreign countries has been for U.S. companies a significant experience for the past one hundred years. But, in long-range historical perspective, the practice is, of course, quite recent. During the age of globalization, overseas trading and mining establishments did indeed assume a global reach, but until the nineteenth century they were confined to territories of one political complexion. Colonial trade and industry were monopolized by the home country. In time, Britain's command of the seas opened increasingly large areas to world trade, but British overseas investment, which supplied and financed a large proportion of the world's initial railroad network and also supported numerous governments through public bonds floated in London, assumed the form largely of portfolio investment and hence of indirect control and left the operation of the projects largely to local or national management. When French and also German financial and industrial interests joined in this activity toward the end of the nineteenth century, they, too, preferred loans and bonds (witness the huge loans to the Russian government, later entirely defaulted); direct investment still tended to be confined to areas under direct political jurisdiction. While multinational business activity was beginning to be introduced, especially in the rising oil

3. British and Canadian companies share some important behavioral characteristics with American corporations—for instance, in the matter of growth rates (Rowthorn with Hymer, 1971: 84), but also in their global involvement, mutual interpenetration, and in financial structure (reliance on stock markets for capital).

industry, in the mining of minerals and in some specialized branches of manufacturing, bonds, stocks, and shares held the predominant share of attention and financiers, the center of the stage. Yet foreign markets were already beginning to be crucial to certain North American corporations: for Standard Oil, even one hundred years ago, or for Singer, whose management inaugurated its first overseas sewing machine factory in Glasgow in 1878. In about 1914, the high point so far of world investment activity, British business held close to one-half the world's foreign investment (Feis, 1931), but, of this, the major part was in stocks and bonds; U.S. investors held less than ten percent, but about half of this was already in direct investment (Wilkins, 1970: 201).

There was not much change in this picture until after World War II, when the field of governmental loans assumed an entirely new character with the creation of the World Bank and the institution of the multifarious mechanisms of foreign aid. Direct foreign investment—that is, the control and operation of business enterprises with branches and subsidiaries in a number of countries—then came into its own with a large outward push by American companies. From about 1950 onward, American firms took advantage of their established knowhow, of favorable political conditions (with the U.S. rise to world leadership), and of advantageous economic circumstances (including the establishment of the dollar as world currency and its later overvaluation). These factors continue to account for the fact that, in the early 1970s, multinational business still is a significantly American-led activity (some 60% in 1965), assuming a proportionately higher share of the global picture than U.S. exports (14.5%) or even U.S. gross product (32.5%).

The role of British finance, still clearly dominant in 1914, had been assumed by American multinationals. But the significance of this process in global proportions should not be exaggerated. In 1914, the grand total of direct foreign investment (say $10 billion in 1914 book values) may have reached perhaps 8 or 10% of the world gross product. By 1965, foreign investment (say $100 billion in 1965 values, nearly two-thirds of it American) may have been less than 5% of world product. Overall, moreover, the salience of foreign investment in U.S. economic activity in 1965 (7.2% of GNP) may have been about the same as in 1897 (8.2%) or 1914 (6.7%). Admittedly, the years before World War I were especially productive of such operations, and foreign investment has never been so salient, before or since. Alarmist views to the contrary, however, multinational business as a whole today is a less dominant, and possibly also a more benign, form of interdependence than it was at the beginning of this century.

Western Europe and Japan

When all of Western Europe (including Britain) is viewed together, its share of multinational business comes to about 30% of the total. At least as many as 40 or 50 European firms may be put in the same category as some 200 large American multinationals. With a few notable exceptions (the British oil companies, and Anglo-Dutch firms, some Swiss producers), these are frequently nationally entrenched companies, rather than firms of a specifically "European" character. Swayed by the example of American giants, they have in recent years become obsessed with size. According to one observer "By the mid-sixties, bigness or gigantism had become a kind of continental fetish" (Sampson, 1971: 125).

Even though, as of about 1965, Japanese overseas investment was quite limited, on the order of 1 or 2% of the world total, Japan now constitutes, principally as the result of high rates of economic growth in recent decades, the third major center of multinationals in the world, and its world share is rising.[4] But this outstanding growth record is not as yet linked with forms of multinational activity made familiar by American experience. As a group, large Japanese corporations apparently have fewer

4 As late as 1965, the largest single national group in the *Fortune* list of non-U.S. industrials was made up of 55 British companies, the second largest being Japanese (34). By 1970, the ranking was reversed; Japanese corporations came first, with 51 entries, while British companies took second place (46).

production facilities outside their home base than comparable American companies. For 22 large Japanese industrial firms (all on the *Fortune* list for 1970)[5] for which the most recent annual reports have been consulted, over one-half had no overseas subsidiaries at all; only three—the very large and independent concerns (Hitachi, Nissan Motors, Matsushita)—had six or more manufacturing establishments overseas. Hardly any Japanese firms approach the level of 25% foreign content of sales or employment that characterizes a significant proportion of American corporations.

A distinguishing feature of Japanese organization is the role of the trading companies, the real "giants" of the economy. Seven of these dominate Japanese merchandising, both domestic and foreign, to the extent that their aggregate sales amount to one-fifth of the GNP. Their function is to take over the marketing, sales, and promotion activities of individual manufacturers, and to serve the great "industrial groups" which organize large parts of the Japanese economy (Mitsui, Mitsubishi, Sumitomo, and the like). Each of the trading companies has extensive networks of overseas offices, associates and also subsidiaries, as one-half of their activities is in foreign trade. As such, they handle large portions of Japan's foreign transactions which, while rising as fast as the GNP, do not loom excessively large in the economy, constituting approximately 20% of GNP (about the world average). The trading companies make it unnecessary for the manufacturers to establish their own subsidiaries and have thus slowed down the evolution of multinational giants. But, in relation to the overseas buyers, the trading companies' sizes give them advantages resembling oligopolistic conditions. This undoubtedly creates another set of problems, but it leaves Japanese companies in a more flexible position in which some of them (such as Komatsu, one hundred-first on the *Fortune* list for 1970), while having no

5. The *Fortune* list is indeed an indispensable tool of research in the field, yet it is not a list of multinational corporations but only of the world's large corporations. Hence, its use tends to direct research toward the study of large firms. The *Yearbook of International Organizations* recently began to publish useful information in the field, too.

subsidiaries, already regard themselves as "world companies" supplying skills to a variety of global customers and exchanging knowledge-based resources throughout the world.

Most multinational business is *produced* in the three core areas of North America, Western Europe, and Japan, which hold about 20% of the world population. But these areas also *consume* the major part of all multinational business acitivity. As judged by the distribution of foreign subsidiaries in the mid-sixties, close to two-thirds of this activity was concentrated in the same areas. The Third World, with nearly one-half the world's people, had the remaining third, and the communist world of the USSR, Eastern Europe, and China (close to one-third of the population) had very little. Thus, neither the production nor even the consumption of the present form of multinational business was truly global in coverage.

There are however, some interesting differences in the types of activity in the developed world and in Third World countries. Overall, and as a world trend, the role of primary and extractive industries in multinational business has been falling. In American foreign investment, it has decreased from more than one-half early in this century, to about one-quarter in the 1960s. Manufacturing and tertiary industries, on the other hand, have been rising, and in Western Europe the bulk of American-based companies are now active in secondary industries and in distribution and services. In the developing countries, however, at least half of foreign investment is still in the extractive industries and a major part of it is concerned with oil.

SIZE OR QUALITY?

The great bulk of multinational activity is still accounted for by a few industries, each controlled by a few large companies. The most important is the oil industry. Standard Oil of New Jersey, the Royal Dutch-Shell Group, Texaco, Gulf, Mobil, and British Petroleum together control close to three-quarters of the free world market in petroleum. Oil alone accounts for some

30% of British foreign investment income, and a large share of French and Italian overseas activity. Next in importance is the automobile industry: General Motors, Ford, Chrysler, Volkswagen, Fiat, British Motors, Nissan, and Toyota dominate world production and account for perhaps another quarter of multinational activity. Altogether, therefore, close to one-half the world's multinational business revolves around the creation and care of motor cars. The third most vital industry, but rising in importance, concerns electronics and the computer, and here the crucial firms include IBM, IT&T, Westinghouse Electric, Philips, Siemens, and Hitachi.

Overall, therefore, a few dozen giants, with a strictly limited range of products, dominate multinational business. But the question may be: must all multinationals be large and so limited in scope? Researchers seem to be making this assumption in deliberate fashion. Vernon has observed (1971: 4, 273) that an enterprise with less than $100 million in sales "rarely merits much attention" and remarked elsewhere that "the possibility that societies may be organized in small units with limited power seems implausible." In consequence, the companies he assembled for study exhibit some extraordinarily impressive features. His 187 multinationals alone accounted for about one-third of the sales and close to one-half the assets of all U.S. enterprises. In addition to extravagant size, the characteristics of his group included great profitability, heavy use of skilled manpower and R & D, and extensive advertising. They were, in short, a group of enterprises "bearing the characteristics usually associated with oligopoly." It may be noted, though, that this conclusion is, in part, the inevitable result of selecting multinationals from the list of large industrials defined by the number of foreign subsidiaries. The question arises whether bigness and, hence, oligopolistic tendencies are inherent qualities of multinationality or rather incidents attributable to the methods used for the selection of firms and the period under investigation. In part, bigness may be a response to uncertainties in the way the world is (or is not) organized. Bigness is, of course, power, and power exerts its own fascination. But at the level of analysis it might be preferable to keep bigness and multinationality separate.

To clarify the use of key terms in this paper, *multinational business* denotes enterprises, and, in particular, corporations, whose business activities are located in a number of nations. Within this broad category, the most attention has so far been paid to the *giant corporations;* these need to be distinguished from enterprises of clearly global purposes, which will be referred to as *global businesses.*

The *giant* customarily is a large national corporation whose activities have spilled over the frontiers of the domestic sphere. It operates extractive and manufacturing facilities in several countries, either in a loose, decentralized manner, or in a tight, centralized way. It employs a considerable labor force, has extensive marketing arrangements in many countries, and deals with a myriad of customers, from countless consumers to governments and other large organizations. Its two distinguishing features are absolute size and operation in a variety of network layers of the world (local, national, and global) in a way which blurs the differences between them and allows opportunities for extensive coordination. General Motors is a standard example of a multinational giant.

Yet the development potential of multinational giants based primarily in the extracting or manufacturing industries, whose "foreign content" consists mainly of equity investment in plants and the organization of labor, may be greatly in doubt. There must surely be room for other types of global firms. Indeed, Richard Robinson (in Brown et al.: 276) has suggested that the international corporation with a bright future is one that specializes in "investing principally in R & D, in the international recruitment and training of skilled technical and managerial personnel, in the organization or interrelated global markets . . . and in the capability of engineering and starting up modern plants, farms, mines, fisheries, schools, hospitals— whatever is needed, so long as ownership is not a precondition." Such companies meet an emerging global need and may rightly be called "global."

Global business is distinguished less by size than by function. It might also take the form of large organizations because worldwide operations call for significant resources, but it need not do so because the efficiency of large-scale structures is often questionable. Typically, such business would specialize in functions requiring worldwide knowledge, a capacity for cross-cultural contacts—hence, also a global identification. It might supply a service which helps the world to function as a unit, operating global networks and acting in fact as a global public utility. INTELSAT is a good example of such a service (Galloway, 1970); international banking and airlines are others. Global businesses might also supply tertiary services based on scarce skills and other intensive capital resources of limited availability even on a global scale, but which are mobile and not bound up with fixed plants and large labor forces. International construction firms, management consultants, companies offering training or prospecting services, firms serving global markets (e.g., in shipping or in some commodities) offer other examples. In the perspective of the future, the globals might be as important as the giants, and they also offer a standard by which the development of the latter might be judged. For it is the function which must be the ultimate criterion of the quality named "multinationality" and not mere size.

Multinationals and War

To determine the contribution of multinational business to world order it is necessary first to explore the thesis, offered by some critics, that multinational business firms contribute to international tensions and war. The evidence for universal involvement in major conflicts in the past has in fact been weak. There have been some spectacular cases of business intervention around the turn of the twentieth century, such as Cecil Rhodes' conquests in Southern Africa, the United Fruit Company's activities in the "banana republics," and oil company ventures in certain parts of the world, including Mexico. But viewed in

global proportions and as an explanatory theory of international politics, the "imperialism" controversy has not had
much factual support for the period prior to 1945. Eugene
Staley (1935) has pointed out that, in some cases, businesses
operating abroad did indeed propel some governments toward
warlike operations, but the instances where governments used
businessmen for their own purposes were just as important.
Lewis Richardson (1960: 60) carefully studied 83 major
conflicts in the period 1820-1929, but found that only three of
these had among their causes economic factors of the type
which included desire for territory as a source of markets and
raw materials. There is only one mention of corporate involvement in war in the entire collection (Standard Oil of New
Jersey in the Chaco War, 1930-1935).

The evidence for the participation of multinational business
(as distinct from business in general) in wars in the period since
1945 is, on the whole, scant. Unlike seventeenth- and eight-
eenth-century trading companies, modern multinational corporations do not field military units (except for security guards)
and so do not engage in military operations. A list of 65
substantial armed conflicts for the period 1945-1970[6] has been
consulted, and a rapid survey does not disclose significant
instances of participation of multinational business in their
causation. Corporate (but not necessarily multinational) in-

6. National wars 1945-1970: Syria-Lebanon, 1945; Greek Civil, 1946-1949;
Bolivia, 1946; Chinese Civil, 1946-1949; Kashmir, 1947-1948; Paraguay, 1947; Israel,
1948-1949; Philippines, 1948-1952; Colombia, 1947-1964; Korea, 1950-1953;
Bolivia, 1952; Quemoy, 1954-1958; Sinai and Suez, 1956; Cuba 1956-1959;
Hungary, 1956; Indonesia, 1957-1961; Lebanon Civil, 1958; Laos, 1959-1962;
Congo, 1960-1965; Nepal Civil, 1960-1962; Bay of Pigs, 1961; Vietnam, 1961- ;
Yemen Civil, 1962-1967; Burundi, 1962; India-China Border, 1962; Guatemala,
1962; Cyprus, 1963-1964; Malaysian Confrontation, 1964-1967; Laos, 1964- ;
Zanzibar, 1964; Dominican Republic, 1965; India-Pakistan, 1965; Indonesia,
1965-1966; Philippines, 1967- ; Six-Day, 1967; El Salvador-Honduras, 1969;
China-USSR Border, 1969; Suez, 1969-1970; Cambodia, 1970- ; Jordan, 1970. Local
wars: Algeria, 1945; Indonesia, 1945-1949; Indochina, 1945-1954; Taiwan, 1947;
Indian Communal, 1947-1948; Madagascar, 1947; Malaysian Emergency, 1947-1952;
Burma, 1952- ; Tunis, 1952; Kenya, 1952-1954; Algeria, 1954-1962; Nagas,
1954-1962; Cameroons, 1956-1961; Cyprus, 1956-1959; Ruanda-Urundi, 1959;
Tibet, 1959; Kurds, 1961-1970; Angola, 1962- ; Aden, 1963-1967; Sudan, 1963- ;
Mozambique, 1965- ; Eritrea, 1965- ; Chad, 1967- ; Biafra, 1967-1970. (Modelski,
1972: 305-306).

terests were involved in the colonial wars in Indonesia (oil, rubber), Malaya (rubber, tin), and Algeria (oil). The clearest instance of a corporate role in international conflict is the intervention of Union Minière du Haut-Katanga (one hundred eighty-third on the *Fortune* list of non-U.S. industrials for 1965) generally in the Congo troubles and in the Katanga secession 1960-1965. Another instance might have been the nationalization of the Suez Canal Company (Anglo-French-owned with strong government participation) which precipitated the events leading up to the Suez war of 1956. Yet another is the discovery and exploitation of sizable oil deposits in Nigeria which had something to do with the onset and the course of the Biafran civil war. In these and other instances, corporate attitudes might have contributed to the hardening of governmental positions, ultimately leading to armed clashes. One case in point was the pressure of oil company interests in relation to Cuba where refineries had been taken over, leading up to the Bay of Pigs landing in 1961. These instances cannot be regarded as proving more than that, in the movement toward the build-up of a conflict, all kinds of interests participate and are brought to bear in one way or another. No case can be made for systematic dominant causative influence.[7]

Documents published in March 1972 by Jack Anderson, the Washington columnist, proved conclusively that some two years earlier, the executives of IT&T (International Telephone and Telegraph Company) discussed, among themselves and with agencies of the federal government, instigating measures to bring about the fall of the Chilean government, possibly by means of a military coup. These plans came to naught, but their publication raised the question whether these are indeed "standard operating procedures" for companies in distress.[8] But here again, an analysis by William Thompson of 274 successful and unsuccessful military coups for the period

7. Similar conclusions emerge from the perusal of a list of 82 incidents of gunboat diplomacy in 1945-1969 (in Cable, 1971: 204-229), only three of which could meaningfully be linked with corporate interests (all in oil).

8. Later in the year, the matter was raised in a United Nations committee and referred to the Secretary-General for study.

1946-1970 generally shows "very little" evidence of "direct involvement" in such activities "on the part of multinational business corporations"—direct involvement being defined as "financial backing and participation in conspiracy planning as well as the unlikely participation in actual military operations."[9] There could conceivably be indirect involvement if and when corporations work through the foreign policy organizations of their home states but, except for the Chilean case which was to be handled by members of the Central Intelligence Agency, and in which a coup neither succeeded nor even materialized, no other case has come to light in any detail. Maybe business corporations are more successful in keeping such matters secret than diplomats or intelligence operators. It might also be noted that a number of coups against company interests are on record too; all four were precipitated by concessions extracted from governments by oil companies: Argentina in 1955, Peru in 1968, Bolivia in 1969, and Iraq in 1969.

Yet another way to test for a relationship between war and multinationals is to relate the incidence of armed conflict to the worldwide distribution of corporate activities. For this purpose, a list of major armed clashes begun or in progress between 1960 and 1970 in various national areas has been compared with the intensity of corporate activities in the same areas, as indicated by the number of corporate associates and subsidiaries about 1966.[10] Thirty-six countries have been identified as conflict locations in that period, and 101 countries as locations of corporate subsidiaries (of 10 and more). Fourteen mostly Western-developed countries, each having between 500 and 2,500 such subsidiaries, show no major conflict location for that period. Eight other countries, in the 250 to 500 subsidiaries range, show 2 conflict areas (Colombia, India). Eighty-seven other, mostly developing countries, each with between 10

9. Private communication April 17, 1972, based on dissertation research, University of Washington.

10. Using data collected in the *Yearbook of International Organizations* for 1968-1969, as compared with 1960-1970 wars in note 6, above.

and 250 subsidiaries, show 22 conflict locations. Some 20 other countries, with less than 10 subsidiaries each, or with none, show 12 more conflict locations. Generally, therefore, high corporate activity goes hand in hand with low conflict incidence; low corporate activity correlates with higher frequency of conflict. The expectation that high corporate involvement brings with it war or armed clashes is not sustained. Upon reflection, this evidence confirms the well-established fact that world business avoids areas of political instability (hence also does not need to concern itself a great deal with war, gunboat diplomacy, or with coups!). It could be argued, of course, that among the causes of political instability is lack of business involvement. But this leads to an altogether different type of argument.

A final test of the relationship between multinationals and war involves the question of corporate involvement in the military-industrial complex—hence, motivation for war preparations. For it has been argued that business benefits from such operations, most tangibly through defense contracts. Can it be shown that multinationals (as distinct from defense contractors in particular and business in general) also participate in large defense contracts and therefore have a stake in rising military expenditures?

The data source at this point is the list of 100 major U.S. defense contractors for fiscal 1968 (at the height of the Vietnam war) which is compared with the established lists of American multinationals (Vaupel and Curhan, 1969: 6-8; Rolfe, 1969: 150-153). Such a comparison shows that the Harvard list of 187 multinationals includes 36 major defense contractors, while the Bruck-Lees list of 81 companies with high (25% or more) "foreign content" has 14 major defense contractors and, therefore, also a slightly lower proportion of companies with large defense contracts.

The conclusion would seem to be (as far as one can judge from American materials in this limited context) that the giants occupy multiple roles and are likely to be both significant defense contractors and also participants in multinational business. The ten largest industrials are also major defense contractors, and nine of them are also multinational (in 1968: GM, Ford, Standard Oil of New Jersey, General Electric, Chrysler, Mobil, Texaco, IBM, Gulf). But below the level of the giants there could be a division of labor developing between more truly domestic companies (such as those engaged in steel and iron and in specific weapons manufacturers) which also specialize in defense work, and others whose business includes significant proportions of foreign sales, earnings, employment, and production, and which tend to be less prominently involved in defense production. Multinationality does not readily go hand in hand with arms production, which involves access to classified information and secret research, security clearances, and other restrictions.[11]

While it is a striking feature of this survey that multinational business as such does not seem to attract violent politics, the only exception to this generalization seems to revolve around primary and extractive industries, including mining—oil mining in particular. Most of the cases of violence (national and local), war, gunboat diplomacy, and coup precipitation on record can be attributed to problems connected with the extraction and utilization of natural resources, of which oil has been the most prominent.

The oil industry, as noted, has been and remains a substantial component of multinational business and, as Barnes' study in this issue shows, it has been notably successful by most business criteria. But the character of multinational business has also been shifting away from extractive activities, toward manufacturing and, indeed, toward tertiary and service functions. These, in the experience of the last few decades, are less likely to arouse national feelings and deep-seated sentiments of national propriety and attachment to the soil. The likelihood of violence centered on territorial rights and the exploitation of the soil could therefore decline, and, by the same token, the need for business to call on the protection of home governments—hence, also their dependence on political support—might wane.

11. But see also the analysis by Galloway, in this issue.

Trends in the evolution of multinational business which are changing its salience and its character are at the same time altering its political complexity and involvement at the level of individual firms. Even for the large oil companies, extraction and even retail marketing are only two among the many global distribution functions in which they might be engaged. But there is another level at which the impact of business on world society may be assessed and that is the structural level of world order. For the argument has been made that international business is a form of imperialism—hence, a special form of foreign domination that by its very nature is conducive to conflict and, if not conflict, then injustice. Hence, even if no single company can be shown to be implicated in violence, the "system" as a whole stands condemned and is judged to be responsible for whatever deficiencies might be attributable to it.

This argument cannot really be proven, but it also is hard to refute; it is not obvious why all the world's discontents should be attributable to this particular form of business organization. But, to the extent that multinational business is one of the principal structural elements of society and giant business its leading and indeed, dominant, part, it must also bear some of the responsibility for its failings. And it is in this sense that the role of multinational business in the making of world order can also be understood.

Two Systems of World Order

What is the role that multinational business plays, not directly, in causing particular wars, but indirectly, through its participation in shaping a world system that tends to break down in violence? Here, association is more difficult to attribute, more speculative in character. A detailed discussion of the influence of multinational business on the strucrure of world politics in the twentieth century might therefore be foregone, in part because the true shape of that factor achieved visibility only in the most recent past.

Questions of the nature of world order are, however, important for all those who are trying to think about the shape of the future, and here clear thinking is more important than history. The following discussion of alternative futures will be conducted in terms of two plausible models of world order: the nation-state system and a world of corporate giants (see also Hymer, 1972). These are 'ideal'-types (in the Weberian sense) which reality need not closely approximate, but they lend structure and set a framework for planning for the future; over a period of time, widespread acceptance of one model as legitimate, or even merely desirable, can have great impact.

THE NATION-STATE SYSTEM

The nation-state system is the most generally accepted principle of world ordering today. Some proponents of multi-national business to the contrary, it is not at all on the verge of disappearing, or of being eroded away under the impact of worldwide corporate activities. It has never in history been as strong as it is at the present time. Governments today annually absorb approximately one-quarter of the world's product; the figure is higher in Europe and is rising in the developing countries.

The rules of the nation-state system are simple, unambiguous, and specify that for every activity, including business activity, the territorial sovereign is the authority in supreme command. Location determines authority and, inasmuch as all the world's land surface is apportioned among a finite number of sovereign states, some government is always known to be in charge.

For economic purposes, the state serves as the coordinator of activity too. It manages demand so as to maintain high employment, regulates the rate of exchange—hence, the terms on which trade will be conducted with nonresidents—and watches over the balance of payments; it mitigates inequalities in income distribution and generally brings the public interest and social control to bear upon a host of business problems. It supervises corporate activity, exacts taxes, influences and even suggests capital formation, generally coordinates many industries by reference to one territorial area, and, in particular, may wish to coordinate national activities with the aim of maximum effectiveness toward outsiders. The most advanced example of the nation-state as economic agent and coordinator is the Communist state, where all economic activity of any significance is subject to central national control. The spectacular growth of the Japanese economy in the last two decades, achieved under national governmental guidance, aided by well-orchestrated foreign trade operations (and creating, for such purposes, what has been dubbed "Japan, Inc.") may represent one other example of the way in which national coordination brings about outstanding results for those who choose to abide by its discipline.

In summary, the advantages of the national system of economic management have included (1) capacity to deal with problems of development in the perspective of the entire nation; (2) ability to correct imbalances in development and to reduce income inequalities and cultural disparities; (3) greater responsiveness to the entire national constituency; and (4) maximization of national advantage toward outsiders.

The weaknesses of the nation-state system are considerable, too, and are most obvious when considered in global perspective:

(1) The system functions best in a situation of autarchy or self-sufficiency. But in conditions of rising interdependence it has no provision for total-system or global coordination; it allows or allocates no resources for the performance of global functions.

(2) Nation-states as presently constituted vary greatly in size and capacity. Few provide a basis for effective economic coordination; many, in fact, only malfunction. Those most in need of coordinated action are those least able to produce it.

(3) Nation-states tend to subordinate economic or welfare considerations to the pursuit of governmental interests, to national security and prestige, and, if unchecked, to expansion. The system has proved incapable of dealing with the problem of war.

(4) In a world of nation-state corporations, some always get ahead of others, but this is a zero-sum process and the world as a whole might actually be worse off: Hence, the need for global coordination.

Indeed, the national-state system, in its competitive aspects (which find expression in such governmental tugs-of-war as arms races, space races, growth and technology gap races, if not in actual war) may be part and parcel of that same super-competitive world process that has created the present structure of wars, as well as monumental global inequalities. These are troubling thoughts. It is such thoughts and criticisms that have prompted many to view the nation-state as an obsolete form of social organization, incapable of mobilizing the resources necessary for the accomplishment of pressing global functions.

A WORLD OF CORPORATE GIANTS

The failings of the nation-state have been obvious, in particular to economists and businessmen raised in the traditions of the free marketplace. The system, by institutionalizing nation-state dominance, is a textbook example of the exploitation of monopoly power in artificially protected jurisdictions. "The nation-state is just about through as an economic unit" wrote Kindleberger (1969: 207) in an echo of George Ball's often-quoted opinion that the nation-state is "a very old-fashioned idea."

Both Kindleberger and Ball were writing in the context of the expanding role of multinational business, a role made possible, in Europe in particular, by the obvious shortcomings of historical nation-states. Frank Tannenbaum put this argument even more boldly: not only is the nation-state becoming "functionless," but the base for an alternative world order is already being formed. This is "the expanding body of international organizations. . . . They are supranational in their very existence, plan and purpose. Their managers, governors, authorities think in extra-national terms; their personnel is indifferent to the nation-state except as an impediment. This extra-national body is the corporation." Its development and future growth is "the major issue confronting mankind" (Brown, 1970: 160-166).

There is a notion abroad that the world is moving rapidly toward a situation where the major part of its industrial output will be dominated by a small number of very large companies (Barber, 1970: part 5; Polk, 1969: 32-33). The calculations and projections underlying this notion are controversial and probably exaggerated.[12] But the vision to which it gives substance is clear and compelling: a world controlled in its economic destinies by 200 or 300 giant concerns (two-thirds of them American) which, in time, will absorb within their compass, through mutual trade and joint ventures, even state-owned industrial administrations in Communist lands. In this world, as Cox (1971) suggests, labor unions too would organize internationally in a coextensive fashion and for bargaining with these giant units, thereby lending them, in fact, additional support.

For analytical purposes, this might be described as a corporation-dominant world order. Corporate dominance would be achieved primarily at the expense of the nation-state and would express itself in an excessive share of the world product absorbed by corporate functions. This would be a "functionalist" world of sorts (Modelski, 1968: 78-79).

Visions of a world of corporate giants tell us not only about the future but also about the present. They show, in the first place, that corporate size has brought with it power that dwarfs many of the nation-states today. With power has also come the ability to generate loyalties, and even ideologies; the ability to create a total institution. A giant multinational can now conceivably offer a focus of loyalty that is competitive with the nation-state. This may be reckoned as a positive contribution to world order; a blurring of frontiers set by states and the evolution of cross-boundary linkages that enrich international life and strengthen the web of interdependence. The corporation's right to relative autonomy may be seen as part of an evolving pluralistic order that has room for a variety of organizational life forms. The existence of such autonomous power centers does not destroy the nation-state, but it does set bounds on claims to a monopoly of power.

Second, the growth of multinational corporations working for the world market demonstrates that maturity has been

12. They depend upon estimates of the size of "international production" which is the output associated with direct foreign investment.

reached by the many organizations now working at the global level. Present-day multinationals are not the first organizations to do so: large navies and oceanic shipping fleets have had such capacity for decades, even centuries. But whereas they functioned at the margin of the world, the multinationals now impinge directly upon great masses of people; the directors of these corporations now command worldwide operations as effectively as the chiefs-of-staff of the military establishment of a great power.

But centralization of control creates complaints about concentration of power and puts into relief problems of responsibility. If decisive world power is, in fact, gathered in the hands of a few corporate leaders, to whom are they accountable? Is this to be a world governed by self-appointed and self-perpetuating cliques of corporate managers? By people who effectively perform their economic functions but are ignorant of or unrelated to wider social problems or global purposes?

We have no means of knowing whether this would be a world without major war. (Who, for instance, would control nuclear weapons?) But other questions of the large framework and the wider purpose remain open. Where do individuals fit in such a world? A system of centralized, multinational giants could not function effectively without a strong political authority. (Yet, this is precluded by definition.) It would be a pure system of pressure groups, unrelieved by any concern for the world public interest. But there still would be need for keeping order, for creating and maintaining rules of corporate interaction and corporate good citizenship. There would be an even stronger need for a global market for public goods that are not provided by corporate initiative. (Who would arrange for moving the garbage, or for cleaning up the world's oceans?) Most importantly, would this also be a just world, sharing advantages fairly among the world's peoples, or would it, in the absence of political mechanisms for redistributing the world's income, no more than confirm the existing divisions between the rich and the poor, the rich areas housing the highly paid corporate headquarters, the top managerial groups, and most of corporate shareholders, and the rest of the world at best a pool of cheap labor and at worst, its stagnant, forgotten, rebellious margins? There is no evidence to show that corporate activity would, in the absence of political mechanisms, in fact, work in a symmetrical fashion and make any contribution at all to ameliorating the world's inequalities of wealth. On the contrary, the last two decades of multinational business growth have coincided with a rise in such inequalities. The provision of such mechanisms, reinforced by world taxation, would drastically alter the character of this system. Without it, it would be unsupportable.

Contrasting with the vision of a world of giant corporations that have lost their national identity is the reality of a contemporary world in which the evidence of international-ization is quite limited. The pressures for centralized operations have set up stresses and political tensions and a good deal of nationalist opposition both in Europe and in the developing areas. But, despite rhetoric, wishful thinking, and some pious wordage, the substantive character of corporations has not changed basically in the past decade. In respect to matters which affect control and responsibility, there have been no changes that would portend an alignment to the requirements of the world interest. In all these aspects, the multinationals in effect remain national; hence, any erosion that has occurred in national control has tended to be one-sided or asymmetrical, at the expense of the weaker governmental structures.

With respect to top management, surveys indicate that the overwhelming proportion remains of the same nationality as the company itself. Vernon (1971: 146) found that all but a trivial fraction of the governing boards and officers of the U.S. parent corporations are U.S. nationals (19 foreigners, including 14 from Britain and Canada, were found in a sample of 1,029 directors). Simmonds (see Brown, 1970: 48-51) obtained quite similar results; among the 150 American corporations surveyed, he found only one or two with more than three members of their top team who were either nonresident foreigners or had transferred after the age of 25. Share ownership shows a similar picture; the foreign portfolio investment in American multi-nationals may be of the order of two or three percent.

No company is significantly linked to a global mechanism of responsibility (an interesting exception being INTELSAT), nor is there much prospect of change in this regard, either in the field of consultation or taxation. In the United Nations, multinational or other corporations have no special role and contribute no inputs, either by way of demands or supports. The I.L.O. is accessible to nationally oriented business leaders, but not to global corporations. The World Bank has no direct link with them, though it has evolved means of consultation on special problems.

Overall, internationalization has had only minuscule impact on multinationals. In fact, the giant companies with numerous subsidiaries have flourished precisely by taking advantage of national frontiers as shelters within which to fashion markets in their own image. Hence, once they penetrate such barriers, they have no incentive to see them taken down and have no difficulty in "going local," on the intermediate management level. Once established, they become beneficiaries of the nation-state system and share some of the accruing benefits with local political leaders who, in their own way, also manage the monopoly of exclusive national politics. Hence, multi-nationals by their very conception thrive upon national divisions and in the decentralized versions of their operations are not incompatible with them at all. They have learnt to live with them and profit by them. Behrman (1969: 121) has found that their officials "generally prefer the contradictions and conflict of the existing multiplicity of jurisdictions and loyal-ties." National sovereignty is not really at bay at all, and the conflict of the multinational corporation with the state is not really as great as it is made out to be.

The world of tomorrow could well be neither a pure nation-state system nor a world of dominant corporate giants, but rather an uneasy compromise between the two. It might be that, for each country and each major area, an equipoise will be reached, in well-known oligopolistic fashion, between sets of large organizations, with strong governments in stand-off accommodation with powerful corporate interests on mutually exclusive spheres of activity. This could be a worse arrangement than either of the two pure types, providing neither peace nor justice, neither change nor competitive innovation; a world that has taken the substance out of innovative growth and that rests content with a ritual of annual style changes as a substitute for real technological development; and the individual might be completely lost sight of.

Be that as it may, it is also clear that the present framework of multinational business formed by giant firms is not a likely seedbed for a world community. But the nation-state is equally inadequate as the sole foundation of world order. While not ignoring these models, constructive thinking will take note of the fact that multinational business itself has been continually changing throughout this century. Such thinking will develop models of world order that do not depend on giant organizations either of the economic or the political type. It will focus research on forms of business activity that perform global functions without overwhelming world structures and that are therefore more likely to be responsive to the world interest.

THE PRESENT ISSUE

Concern with conditions of world order, in particular as affected by relations between governments and business, and by the impact of global corporations on society, is the thread running through this entire issue of the *Quarterly*.

The two contributions that follow this opening essay focus on the form and substance of relations between multinational enterprises and national authorities. Boddewyn and Kapoor reveal how an entire sector of corporate management now specializes in dealing with governments and other public bodies. Barnes' paper analyzes the experience of the world's two major oil companies in their dealings with governments when facing a variety of forms of wealth deprivation, including expropriation, over a period of fifty years. This is long enough to permit some confident generalizations about the staying power of these organizations. Both papers in effect show how successfully large companies cope with governments. Fayerweather's question-naire survey of Britain, Canada, and France complements these studies by displaying evidence that corporate activities, at any rate in those three countries, are grounded in broadly favorable attitudes of national governing elites.

The last three papers examine, from different vantage points, the impact of large corporations on the world, and on world order at large. Galloway studies the evidence bearing on linkages between the defense establishment and multinational corpora-tions in the United States; his analysis shows these linkages to be significant in the case of some companies and some industries. Ajami points to some important social costs of the multinational giants that have emerged through the process of global economic concentration. As a student of political theory, von Krosigk, finally, reminds us that Marxist scholars have a long tradition of reflecting on these matters going back to Marx himself, and that Lenin's well-known views represent only one strand of Marxist thought on the political consequences of worldwide business organizations.

The issue brings together a variety of viewpoints and approaches. It is intended to inform and to raise issues of interest to students of international relations; it was also designed to afford an outlet for current research of a number of styles, methods, and perspectives. It shows that the activities of multinational corporations form a significant and growing field of interest, that interesting work is now in progress, and that a fuller and richer understanding of the global system is likely to result from it.

REFERENCES

BALL, G. (1967) "The promise of the multinational corporation" Fortune 75 (June 1): 80.
BANNOCK, G. (1970) The Juggernauts: The Age of the Big Corporation. London: Weidenfeld.
BARBER, J. (1970) The American Corporation. New York: G. P. Dutton.

BEHRMAN, J. (1970) National Interests and the Multinational Enterprise. Engle-
wood Cliffs, N.J.: Prentice-Hall.
——— (1969) Some Patterns in the Rise of the Multinational Enterprise. Chapel Hill:
University of North Carolina Graduate School of Business Administration.
BERTIN, G. (1972) L'investissement international. Paris: Presses Universitaires de
France.
BROWN, C. [ed.] (1970) World Business: Promise and Problems. New York:
Macmillan.
BROWN et al.
CABLE, J. (1971) Gunboat Diplomacy: Political Applications of Limited Naval
Force. New York: Praeger.
COX, R. (1971) "Labour and international relations." International Organization 25
(Autumn): 554-584.
FEIS, H. (1931) Europe, the World's Banker 1870-1914. New Haven, Conn.: Yale
Univ. Press.
Fortune (1969) "The challenge of international business" Volume 80 (August 15):
27-28.
GALLOWAY, J. (1970) "World-wide corporations and international integration: the
case of Intelsat." International Organization 24 (Autumn): 503-519.
HELLMANN, R. (1970) The Challenge to U.S. Dominance of the International
Corporation. New York: Dunellen.
HYMER, S. (1972) "The multinational corporation and the law of uneven
development," in J. N. Bhagwati (ed.) Economics and World Order. New York:
Macmillan.
KINDLEBERGER, C. (1969) American Business Abroad. New Haven, Conn.: Yale
Univ. Press.
MACRAE, N. (1972) "The future of international business" Economist 242, 6700:
v-xxxvi.
MAGDOFF, H. (1969) The Age of Imperialism. New York: Monthly Review Press.
MODELSKI, G. (1972) Principles of World Politics. New York: Free Press.
——— (1968) "The corporation in world society." Year Book of World Affairs 22:
64-79.
MOON, P. T. (1930) Imperialism and World Politics. New York: Macmillan.
PECCEI, A. (1971) "Will businessmen unite the world?" Center for the Study of
Democratic Institutions Occasional Papers, Santa Barbara, California, April.
POLK, J. (1969) "The rise of world corporations." Saturday Rev. 52 (November 22):
32-34.
RICHARDSON, L. (1960) Statistics of Deadly Quarrels. Pittsburgh: Boxwood.
ROLFE, W. (1969) The International Corporation. Istanbul. International Chamber
of Commerce.
ROWTHORN, R. with S. HYMER (1971) International Big Business, 1957-1967.
London: Cambridge Univ. Press.
SAMSON, A. (1971) The New Europeans. London: Panther.
SCHUMPETER, J. (1951) "Imperialism," in Imperialism: Social Classes. New York:
World.
STALEY, E. (1935) War and the Private Investor. Garden City, N.Y.: Doubleday.
VAUPEL, J. W. and J. P. CURHAN (1969) The Making of Multinational Enterprise.
Boston: Harvard Business School.
VERNON, R. (1971) Sovereignty at Bay. New York: Basic Books.
WILKINS, M. (1970) The Emergence of Multinational Enterprise. Cambridge, Mass.:
Harvard Univ. Press.

The External Relations of American Multinational Enterprises

J. BODDEWYN and ASHOK KAPOOR

Graduate School of Business Administration
New York University

The Nature and Necessity of External Relations

Business corporations need to engage in external relations (ER) because society must be continuously convinced to give and maintain its support of this man-made and socially tolerated instrument for organizing economic activity and to stop short of unduly restraining it.

Society here refers to the more or less organized and powerful institutions and interest groups that can assist or hamper business in its economic role. Government is usually the most relevant "external" institution but it is more or less influenced by interest groups and by the more amorphous general public. These various collectivities constitute the "non-market" and "macro-managerial" environments of business, which are distinct from the relatively free "markets" for the firm's inputs and outputs, and from its internal "micro-management." Hence, *external relations (ER) is that function*

AUTHORS' NOTE: This article is part of a larger ongoing study by the authors on the nature and characteristics of international external relations by large American companies. This study made for the American Management Association is based on extensive field research in Western Europe and Asia. More than 250 interviews with corporate executives in New York City and in these regions were conducted in 1970, 1971, and early 1972.

[31]

of the firm concerned with enlisting the support or negating the opposition of those nonmarket and macro-managerial collectivities that actually or potentially affect its existence and prosperity. [1]

Thus defined, external relations differs from public relations as the latter is generally conceived and conducted nowadays. Whether rightly or wrongly, PR has come to evoke the lower-level handling of press releases by slick publicity agents. On the other hand, external relations (or public affairs or corporate affairs) has been deliberately chosen by a growing number of firms in order to emphasize three important distinctions: (1) it is fundamentally a top-line management function, whether or not there is a lower-level technical staff to assist it; (2) it is more than a matter of "relations," but also concerns "intelligence"—hence, the increasing preference for the term "affairs" rather than "relations"; and (3) it involves a broader variety of targets than the public and more than its reaching through mass media.

More specifically, external relations deals with: (1) government in its multiple roles as legitimizer, regulator, promoter, competitor, partner, supplier, and customer; (2) the trade-union movement as a countervailing power group; (3) trade and professional associations as well as the rest of the industry in its noneconomic roles; (4) the intellectual, moral, and scientific communities; and (5) public opinion at large.

Each of these subgroups is obviously not watertight because of overlapping memberships. Besides, not all these relations of the firm with outside institutions and groups are of the external type, properly speaking, because they also deal with them in more normal "business" relationships. Thus, the unions supply labor after rounds of bargaining; the universities provide research and training; the trade associations make various statistics and information available; and the government buys and sells certain goods and services. Such activities are correctly

1. External relations is concerned mainly with the broad political, social, and cultural dimensions of the firm's economic task and performance—with what Parsons (1960: 63-64) calls the "institutional" or "community" level of an organization.

subsumed under the more traditional categories of industrial relations, engineering, marketing, and the like, even though they may well affect the firm's external relations.

Finally, some element of significance or discretion must be introduced in the concept of external relations. Take the matter of government relations, which will provide the main focus of this paper, other groups being mostly considered to the extent that they affect the former. Many firms sell to and buy from the government, file reports, pay taxes, obtain permits, borrow from state-owned banks, avail themselves of investment incentives, use public training facilities, obey or disobey laws, and consume government services on a purely routine basis. Only when some discretionary and significant action is exercised on either side will it be considered as falling within the scope of external relations.

The Internationalization of External Relations

If external relations constitutes an intrinsic function for all organizations—be it only in the form of some deliberate or implicit low profile—then it follows that international business firms also engage in them. For that matter, a growing number of American multinational enterprises (MNEs)[2] are institutionalizing the function by creating staff positions for that purpose at various geographic levels, and their line executives are becoming more involved in external relations.

CAUSAL FACTORS

The most obvious explanation for this recent emergence is that ER represents a countermove to the MNEs under attack, as their number, size, impact, and visibility have grown. These developments are of concern to many national governments,

2. There is much debate about the meaning of the expression "multinational enterprise." Without entering into this debate, we are referring to large organizations with significant and growing international involvement. For additional discussion, see Kapoor and Grub (1972).

firms, unions, and others who feel challenged by the MNEs' relative power and independence, particularly in the context of resurgent nationalism.[3] Firms then must defend themselves against various criticisms (real, false, or exaggerated) and reactions (regulations, expropriations, strikes, boycotts and the like).

Abroad, business has long been challenged by socialist, nationalist, corporativist, and other schemes. The MNE is thus even more under siege than the purely domestic firm, and it must be particularly careful to make its contributions to the respective national interests evident, to minimize the impact of conflicts of sovereignties, and to avoid clashes with nationalistic feelings. It is the very matter of acquiring legitimacy—particularly within the host society—that is at stake, and this is normally more difficult for a foreign than a domestic enterprise to achieve.

A less dramatic explanation of the development of external relations is that what is done overseas largely reflects domestic practice. The firm that is active in ER in its home country is more likely to be involved abroad also. Since ER problems are growing in the United States, the acquired expertise is increasingly available for transmittal overseas. Besides, the problems of the parent company increasingly follow its traveling offspring. Thus, the Dow Chemical office in Frankfurt was bombed as a protest against its napalm-making activities in the United States; while Union Carbide people in Europe got calls from the press and inquiries from various communities right after their pollution problems in West Virginia were aired in the American press. Demonstrations, physical assaults, boycotts, and general harassment of American subsidiaries has occurred in many developing countries—notably in the Philippines, Peru, India, and Chile. Overseas subsidiaries must then follow suit and engage in external relations.

Yet, external relations abroad do not simply mirror the level of involvement at home because, in many cases, *more* ER is

3. There is an extensive and excellent literature to that effect by such scholars as Raymond Vernon, Richard D. Robinson, Jack N. Behrman, John Fayerweather, and Charles P. Kindelberger.

needed outside the United States. The reasons for this situation are fairly complex but can be reduced to two major ones. First, foreign governments by and large play a more active role in the economy than in the United States. If nothing else, this calls for a good deal of *defensive* action on the part of the MNE. Beyond that, however, foreign governments often invite close relationships between the state and business in the context of economic planning, industrial policy, regional development, the consultative function, industrial relations, and the like. *Positive* action is indicated, too, because such association with government creates various opportunities for influencing government policy and action, be it for mercenary or enlightened purposes.

Second, there is often more collective action or "concertation" abroad among business firms, within trade associations, and with labor and other interest groups. Such involvements in collective action are sometimes mandatory (e.g., the Chambers of Commerce and Industry in various countries) and often highly desirable. The American subsidiary has to fit into such a "corporativistic" milieu through various forms of external relations (Boddewyn et al., 1972).

INTERNATIONAL DIMENSIONS

While it is easy to visualize each American subsidiary overseas dealing with its *domestic* environment, there is also a true *international* dimension to external relations that goes beyond the local level.

(1) United States-foreign country. Some action of the parent company in the United States or of the American government, even when purely local in character, can have rapid ER repercussions abroad. For example, the U. S. government forces a pharmaceuticals firm to withdraw some prescription item from the market, and this product soon no longer qualifies for reimbursement under several foreign social security systems.

This kind of involvement requires that the parent company be aware of the actual or potential repercussions of its activities and be equipped to inform and otherwise assist its subsidiaries abroad. Conversely, the parent firm must be cognizant of and able to react to foreign developments likely to affect its U. S. external relations (e.g., on account of continuing operations in Rhodesia, South Africa, and Greece, following the advent of "reactionary" governments).

(2) Foreign country-foreign country. Action taken in one foreign nation can affect another, and thus lead to external relations problems. For example: American firms are often investigating several neighboring countries simultaneously in the process of choosing factory or office sites. Such concurrent negotiations must be coordinated and skillfully handled lest the spurned governments retaliate against the company by hampering the importation of its products or by not ordering them for their own state agencies and enterprises.

This kind of external relations problem obviously requires some coordination either by the international headquarters or by a regional office. It is gaining in importance because host governments are beginning to cultivate a dialogue, especially with their neighbors, through regional organizations such as the Economic Commission for Asia and the Far East, and the Organization for Economic Cooperation and Development.

(3) The Supranational level. The true MNE is often said to be ahead of governments and other institutions when it comes to organizing itself on a regional or world level. However, there are already supranational bodies that require attention. An increasing number of firms are watching the European Economic Community and the Central American Common Market—among others—because of their existent, incipient, or potential regulatory or moral powers. Besides, many developing countries turn to the United Nations and its numerous agencies for general and specific assistance in formulating technical codes for industries and other areas of activities influencing private enterprise, both domestic and foreign.

Besides being watched, such bodies must also be informed of the MNE's views and problems. Most supranational institutions are understaffed, yet are expected to take stands or measures that affect international trade and investment. Hence, an increasing number of regional headquarters follow the activities of, and feed information to, these organizations, as well as to country representatives serving on them.

(4) The Global level. In view of the frequent observation that the nation-state is obsolete and that a few hundred giant MNEs will eventually produce and market most of the world's goods and services, one could imagine that some "global" thinking, planning, and organizing is already fairly common in large internatioanl firms. However, neither these premises nor the derived conclusion is correct. As Modelski (1971: 25-26) points out, the nation-state and nationalism are alive and well, and the MNEs are not necessarily hampered by their survival and strength—in fact, they are often the beneficiaries of the nation-state system.

Besides, external relations is rather "polycentric" in nature; that is, it must carefully espouse the characteristics of the environment where it is carried out.[4] Hence, there is still relatively little which can be contributed by the parent company or the international headquarters. This situation, however, is bound to change as exchangeable experience is obtained both at home and abroad, and as supranational institutions develop. Besides, the role of the world HQ is growing because of instantaneous communications which require quick uniform responses in many overseas locations, because of the precedent-setting effects of the decisions of other governments which demand coherent reactions, and because of the apparent trend toward more centralization within MNEs.

---

4. This is one of the three key concepts developed by H. V. Perlmutter. The *ethnocentric* firm considers that the parent company and country know best, and they do therefore impose their ways abroad; the *polycentric* pattern is based on the acceptance that foreign countries are different and thus warrant tailor-made "local" solutions; while the *geocentric* firm seeks a blending of the best solutions wherever they come from.

Factors Affecting the ER Structure

In view of these considerations, it is easy to envision all MNEs with large ER staffs at various levels. In fact, the majority of American international corporations are like the one whose vice president said: "We deal with external relations on an ad hoc basis because we are not a large company; it is not a company tradition; the government is not a customer of ours; and we are not particularly regulated." The stakes are thus not equal, and neither are the responses. Still, ER staffs are emerging for a variety of reasons, small and large, whose cumulative effect is to increase awareness by senior line management of the need for such an apparatus, as well as to accelerate its development.

COMPANY TRADITION, RESOURCES, AND POLICY

As a first approximation, a subsidiary's involvement in external relations tends to reflect that of the parent company, even though the need may be greater overseas. However, for some fairly large U. S. firms, ER is not a company tradition or policy, and only a handful of line executives at corporate headquarters are aware of the need for developing a staff. Many others believe that low profile external relations is best, or they simply prefer to concentrate on short-term profit considerations, thereby minimizing the need for ER activities which, almost by definition, are of a long-term nature.

More generally, as Behrman (1971: 228) points out, communication between business and the U. S. government in matters of international economic policy (among others), has not been particularly well structured or fruitful; this does not predispose American subsidiaries abroad to pay much attention to systematic and long-term, objective-oriented relations with governments in host countries. Other aspects of external relations may be better developed, however, as in community relations about pollution, where the pressure is more immediate.

Some industries have a much longer ER tradition. This is particularly the case in the petroleum, pharmaceutical, and telecommunications fields, where government relations have always been very important. For a few companies, it is a matter of deliberate policy, as in the case of IBM, where, aside from any immediate external problems, the company has progressively encompassed stockholders, then employees and customers, and now the community at large among its concerns.

SIZE, AGE, AND GROWTH

Larger subsidiaries tend to be more involved in external relations than smaller ones, because their impact and visibility are greater. Moreover, greater size means that more resources are available and influence is more likely and even expected.

However, it is well to realize that, for all the talk about giant MNEs roaming around the world, many American companies and plants abroad are rather small. Obviously, some firms loom very large (e.g., IBM, ITT, and the petrochemical companies), but even some of the large ones are not that big, relatively speaking. In 1968, the average American enterprise in Belgium had only 337 employees; and in Asia the average investment by an American company is less than $1 million. Of course, what is considered small in the American context may be viewed as rather large abroad; and a plant manager may have sizeable community relations, particularly if it is a one-company town or if there are local problems in such matters as pollution. One must also realize that, in a foreign country, this "plant" is a "firm," both *legally* (since most firms are incorporated, rather than branches) and *symbolically,* as it represents a foreign company.

There is no ready pattern as far as age is concerned. Obviously, with age comes experience, and this may lead to more and better developed external relations. Regarding growth, as American firms become larger overseas and as U. S. investments grow in a particular country, they draw more attention, both favorable and unfavorable. Thus, conflicts as well as cooperative endeavors with governments become more likely as both legal enforcement and economic policy tend to focus on the larger firms. The rest of the industry and the trade association also grow more aware of American competition for labor, capital, raw materials, and markets. The unions turn out to be more demanding once the foreign employers have exhausted the local labor pool that often attracted them in the first place (union leaders are often told or can figure out for themselves that it is better not to "scare" the Americans at first); and they are increasingly trying to develop multicountry labor negotiations and to restrict the logistical shifting of production from one subsidiary to another. The press and the intelligentsia more and more report on the MNE (mostly the foreign ones); and, according to some Gresham's law, bad news tends to crowd out good news when such a coverage expands. All these elements result in the public paying more attention to foreign companies, particularly in countries with a colonial history. Consequently, external relations become increasingly necessary to cope with these publics that loom larger as the firms develop or the awareness of their presence grows.

TYPE OF INDUSTRY

Some industries have more ER problems than others. Pharmaceuticals, for example, are heavily supervised in many countries where social security systems provide free or cheap prescriptions for everybody but where governments want to keep down the price of prescriptions. This is also an industry which must repeatedly explain the large spread between direct production costs and final prices and justify the payment of sizeable foreign royalties. (Petroleum companies have a similar problem in the matter of transfer pricing.) Pharmaceuticals also represent a type of industry where a complex set of relations must be built with various departments and advisory commissions within national governments and international bodies (e.g., the EEC); with universities from which come some of the research and many of the experts who comment on new formulas and pricing proposals; and even with suppliers (e.g., chemical firms) and consumers (pharmacists and hospitals).

Extraction is, of course, the prototype of an industry with major external relations problems because of the strong nationalistic emotions associated with natural resources. However, a "dirty" industry is also vulnerable nowadays, and there are strong prejudices everywhere against pure marketing firms because the importation of foreign products is seen as taking jobs away from local workers, and because distribution is generally seen as a parasitic function (unless it is for exports). Other industries, however, have much less visibility, particularly if they are industrial suppliers. Thus, Eaton has recently been advertising that it probably is "the largest multinational corporation you have never heard of!"

CRISES

Some firms do not lock the barn until after the horse has been stolen. Thus, IBM World Trade got to straighten certain communication lines with the American government only after the fracas created when the State Department forbade the sale of a high-powered computer to the French government. For other firms, it may be a badly handled case of pollution, transfer pricing, or layoff; a matter of the press quoting some damaging facts; or of an opposition party trying to embarrass the government.

Not all these troubles end up badly. Thus, an American pharmaceutical firm in Europe was erroneously criticized in a newspaper article for not listing abroad certain contraindications on its labels, as it did in the United States. At first, this hurt sales badly; but it led the firm to contact medical journalists and to be interviewed on TV and radio, which gave it some good exposure. Besides, the Health Ministry felt criticized, too, and came to the defense of the company, thereby creating a closer rapport between the firm and its major regulator and customer.

A firm may also get involved in external relations when other American companies create crises. Thus, it takes a long time to live down a badly handled case of pulling out of a foreign country, as when Raytheon left Sicily in a hurry and when a consortium of oil and chemical companies withdrew its offer for organizing a massive fertilizer-manufacturing capacity to the government of India. This is a case where American Chambers of Commerce abroad can help, but they require prodding, financing, and assisting—all legitimate ER activities.

A related case of getting into ER on account of others is when American subsidiaries abroad have to match, or at least keep track of, what their competitors are doing in the way of lobbying, trade-association leadership, public-opinion campaigns, relations with universities, and so on. For example, the Indian government was debating in 1967 a patents bill which would have had serious implications for foreign companies operating in India. These firms had to seek the support of their trade associations in India in order to lobby more effectively with agencies and officials of the Indian government.

Furthermore, all over the world, concern is growing and widely shared about pollution, consumer protection, the "military-industrial complex," the hiring of minorities and women, the dehumanizing effect of work, or the exploitation or ignoring of poor countries—however real or soluble these problems may be. Besides, there are the older but still potent issues of ensuring employment security and work safety, to mention just a few. Companies are now expected to know, care, do, and tell more and better. Companies that sought a low profile are thus progressively dragged into the limelight; being an "alien" does not permit a foreign company to maintain a low profile easily or to be measured by standards of behavior applied to indigenous enterprises.

OVERALL COMPANY STRUCTURE

There are three fundamental ways of organizing a company: (1) on a functional basis (production, marketing, finance, research and development, control, and so on); (2) on a geographic basis (by country or region); and (3) by product. Many organization structures are hybrid or frequently altered for a variety of personal, organizational, and environmental reasons. Besides, companies organized on either a functional or product basis often have an "International Division" that assists or coordinates overseas exports, investments, licenses, contracts, and the like. Furthermore, whatever the organization basis chosen, international firms have varying philosophies regarding the desirable autonomy of their foreign affiliates.

Favoring the *geographic* basis is the fact that external relations (like advertising and industrial relations) is a polycentric function closely related to the idiosyncrasies of each national environment. In any case, outside the public relations and scientific relations parts of ER, American parent companies do not have that much experience to contribute to foreign subsidiaries. This tends to nip any "ethnocentric" tendencies in the bud; while it is still too early to develop a "geocentric" approach on account of the newness of most of the solutions developed around the world.

The *product* basis appears less favorable to external relations because it is usually associated with a centralized structure to which the ER function does not lend itself readily. An additional layer of staff functions (including ER) must then be superimposed on the product structure; and various coordinating mechanisms must be introduced when several product divisions operate in the same country or region. Yet, it is also a type of organization structure partial to joint ventures which facilitate under certain conditions the performance of external relations via the local partner who may even assume complete responsibility for ER when products are sold under his name.

The *functional* basis of organization occupies an intermediary position in this respect. Largely limited to single-product companies, it resembles the product-based structure but without the complication created by many products. It is more likely, however, to be ethnocentric in attitude and thus less amenable to "national" or "regional" solutions than the geographic structure.

Conglomerate firms—such as ITT, which is involved in a large variety of activities such as telecommunications (both manufacturing and operations), hotels, car rental, housing development, and foods—have special problems because no single basis for organization structure is completely suitable. It is worth noting, however, that this complexity has not prevented ITT from being very active in the ER field.

Shifting from one organizational form can be troublesome, however. Thus, reorganizing a geography-based MNE on a product basis can jeopardize years of effort spent in building constructive relationships with key government executives and other influential elites—particularly in less-developed nations where personal relations are quite important. Similarly, developing a footloose "geocentric" corporation that moves its production facilities around the world as costs and markets shift is likely to create sizeable external relations problems, as is well evidenced by U. S. labor's and Congress' recent reactions to firms building plants abroad rather than in the United States (or even closing down U. S. plants in this context).

The ER function itself can affect the choice of structure because good external relations may preclude a more centralized structure. Thus, there is no ITT-France because ITT is a conglomerate which includes several major manufacturers of telecommunications equipment sold mainly to the French government. It prefers to be seen buying from apparently "local" firms, which are often acquisitions or former licensees that have retained their former local names. Such an obstacle does not exist in the case of other ITT subsidiaries such as Sheraton and Avis, where the very fact of belonging to an international network is a positive marketing asset and of little "nationalistic" importance.

OUTSIDE RESOURCES

What ER tasks need to be performed internally is partly a function of the availability of external sources of information, assistance, and influence. The United Kingdom, for example, has a first-rate economic press which simplifies the task of collecting and interpreting information about a number of problems. The spread of such worldwide intelligence services as Business International is also useful in this respect. In some countries, there are excellent international law firms as well as banks and engineering firms to guide prospective investors about approaching governments, and international public relations services are becoming more readily available. Practically everywhere there are "consultants" of various backgrounds (including ex-Prime Ministers, generals, and members of parliament) and capabilities ready to assist in ER matters. Such services must obviously be appraised, used, and coordinated by knowledgeable persons, but their very availability allows firms to function with a lighter ER structure than if they had to do all or most of it—as is more often the case in less-developed countries.

External Relations: Line or Staff?[5]

A TOP-MANAGEMENT FUNCTION

Even when there is an ER staff, a good part of external relations cannot be delegated to staff people or even to lower-level executives, but must be handled by line people at the very top. The first and more fundamental reason for this situation is that the acquisition of legitimacy and community support (typically bestowed by government, public opinion, and other "legitimizing" groups such as the scientific and intellectual community, labor, the rest of the industry, and the banking system) must be handled at the very top because nobody else can represent the corporation in this search (Parsons, 1960; Parsons and Smelser, 1956).

5. In classical terms, the *line* executives are vested with the primary source of authority, while the *staff* supports and advises the line. This delineation is obviously not always clear as when staffs are given "functional" authority to control (singly or in tandem with other line executives) the activities of some lower-level line or staff members of the organization. Thus, the ER staff in the parent company may either "advise" or "control" the ER staff in the foreign subsidiaries, besides advising the line executives in the parent or subsidiary companies.

Normally, this task is carried out by the board of directors, and some American subsidiaries abroad use it for that purpose, particularly when local nationals must sit on such boards (as in Sweden and Japan). However, most U. S. subsidiaries have only nominal boards of directors composed of executives from headquarters and the local firm. This means that, for all practical purposes, this institutional task of acquiring legitimacy and support has to be handled by the top executive(s) on the spot, whether consistently or on an ad hoc basis.

Another more practical reason why external relations cannot be delegated downward is that, as one executive put it: "Only real power can face power" in important negotiations and deliberations with government and other groups. Staffs and lower-level managers can obviously prepare the ground and carry out routine or less crucial transactions; but only the man or men who know and represent the total firm and control its resources can speak with full authority when important matters are at stake.

This requirement is reinforced by the fact that, in Europe and many developing countries, there is a long tradition of centralized authority whereby companies speak only through their top executives. Having a lesser executive represent the company in major external matters is actually interpreted as a slur toward the other party and is not conducive to open and productive deliberations. Protocol thus also requires top-management involvement in external relations.

STAFF OR NO STAFF?

The fact that top-line executives must concern themselves directly with the management of external relations and even participate in their execution does not preclude the existence of a supporting staff of specialists. Most firms provide for such support although the majority do not have any full-fledged ER staff (of whatever size) but only part-time assignees.

When the factors conditioning the relative importance of the ER function rate low (e.g., size, tradition, involvement with government), there is usually no staff. However, even large subsidiaries have cause for moving slowly toward creating an ER staff for lack of relevant models to copy, and for fear of overdoing the whole thing. As one regional ER director put it: "One cannot delegate this function without inflating it out of proportion to what can really be done at levels lower than the top, and without ending up with busybodies claiming they do all sorts of useful things."

Another element favoring a small staff or no staff at all is that part of this function is carried out by other people and units within and without the firm. Thus, some of the relations with government pass through the legal, financial, accounting, and marketing sides (e.g., taxes, customs classification); production and engineering people get involved in trade-association committees dealing with such matters as industrial standards, and they handle part of the relations with the scientific community; some of the relations with employers' associations and the labor movement are handled by the industrial relations department, and so on. Clearly, this diffusion calls for coordination and common servicing, but it remains that all external relations do not have to pass through a specialized internal staff.

An additional shortcut consists of using the ER services of a "big sister" company. This approach is common in petrochemicals, where the petroleum company is considered to be the ER expert; or when one subsidiary is designated as the "senior company" in a particular country. Some joint ventures abroad also use the ER expertise of the local partner.

Companies can also avail themselves of the external services of banks, law and CPA firms (domestic and international), public relations consultants, trade associations, American and local Chambers of Commerce, and U. S. embassies who provide information, advice, or introductions, or may even carry out certain negotiations for the firm.

Finally, some ER activity is built into other measures, such as the appointment of a local national as general manager, the technical upgrading of the local workforce, or the entering into joint ventures with local partners (private and public). Such very important ways of acquiring legitimacy do not require any ER staff—only the appropriate ER mentality.

A sizeable number of firms already have an ER staff, although not necessarily at all levels, since the major problems, interests, and resources may only be present at either the local, national, regional, or world level, and because one level (e.g., the region) may be the most appropriate for learning about external relations and educating the rest of the organization.

The ER Men

Like many other functions in a business organization, the ideal qualifications for ER work are not clear-cut, nor are the arrangements perfect. Some patterns are observable, however.

THE "ADVISERS"

Companies sooner or later turn to outsiders for ER advice on a paying (e.g., consultants and lawyers), reciprocal (e.g., banks, U. S. embassies, local partners, competitors, other American firms abroad), or casual basis. Some of this advice is obtained in the context of other activities (e.g., in discussing some financing with a banker, a contract with a lawyer, or a procedure with bureaucrats); but ER assistance may also be sought for its own sake in the context of planning, reporting to higher levels in the company, and of "monitoring" the environment.

Thus, one American company asked a former European Prime Minister's opinion about how to inform the present government of its purchase of a major local firm (no permission was required, and he advised them to present the government with a fait accompli, but to inform it before anybody else). In another vein, briefing sessions by the U. S. ambassador or conferences organized by a trade association or by the American Chamber of Commerce are often mentioned as ways of keeping up with significant developments, besides what the general and specialized press have to say on these subjects.

A smaller proportion of American firms have internalized such advising at various levels. Thus, active and retired political figures often serve on the Boards of Directors of large companies. The legal counsel and other functional specialists are also major sources of advice—either generally or about special problems such as likely tax changes, forthcoming labor regulations, or an unfavorable article in the press.

Such advising has no nationality, as good advice is accepted from anyone, even though an American source can sometimes better relate to the mentality of the U. S. advice-seeker.

THE "DOOR OPENERS"

Sometimes overlapping with the advisers, this group is made up of people that have "connections" by family ties, social position, education, or previous employment (e.g., a former Filipino senator or a French "Inspecteur des Finances"). Local nationals may have been recruited, partly because they possess such a marketable asset, besides being qualified to serve in some other capacity, while other firms simply discovered that they had such people on the payroll. Some U. S. international law and public relations firms may also serve as door openers.

THE "DOERS"

This group is made up of those who make and execute policy in the ER field. We saw earlier that this is a function from which top management cannot divorce itself, be it only to conclude that the company has few problems in this area or should adopt a low profile. The problem here is that frequently the general manager's experience may have poorly prepared him for external relations—a difficulty often compounded by his lack of familiarity with the country's environment.

Outside major negotiations for investing in the country, it appears that indigenous general managers are better equipped to fill the external relations role because they have a more innate understanding of the milieu, but this should not be automatically assumed. After all, did the average American manager in the United States spot or react fast to such issues as the anti-war protest, environmental protection, women's rights, the youth culture, or even consumerism? Besides, many American subsidiaries abroad are small and not deeply involved with their environment. Hence, an American can handle the ER function quite well, with the help of some of his subordinates. Needless to say, the general manager, to be effective, must be perceived as having real authority, without his being connected to Detroit or New York via a telex machine.

It is not uncommon to find most or part of the ER task delegated to a personal assistant to the general manager when the company needs to be active in this field. Such assistants are typically nationals who have (or are supposed to have) particular ER skills, including good connections. Thus, one American subsidiary in the pharmaceutical field has a personal assistant to the president who is a pharmacist, a teacher in several universities, a deputy mayor, a county councilman, a member of various consultative bodies and trade associations, and a consultant to government.

Some firms use full-time or part-time lobbyists as doers (rather than as advisers or door-openers) but not as much as might be expected—the main reason being the fear of loss of control over their activities.

Conclusion

The large majority of U. S. multinational firms are becoming aware of the importance of the ER function, and the forces which have created this awareness (nationalism, environmental concern, public criticism, management sophistication) will remain in effect in the coming years. This will result in a stronger tendency on the part of a growing number of companies to progress toward more formal organization structures than is the case at present. Also, a growing body of precedents in other organizations will simplify the decision by any one company to formulate systematic ER action programs.

Foreign companies exist in given countries at the will of the host government; and as host governments and other societal groups (e.g., the intelligentsia) become more sophisticated in their understanding of multinational business, the demands on the MNE will also grow. Consequently, effective external relations will continue to be an essential requirement for international business operation.

REFERENCES

BEHRMAN, J. (1971) U. S. International Business and Governments. New York: McGraw-Hill.

BODDEWYN, J. (1969) "Don't take Belgium for granted." Worldwide P & I Planning (November-December): 39-49.

――― et al. (1972) World Business Systems and Environments. Scranton, Pa.: International Textbook.

KAPOOR, A. (1970a) International Business Negotiations: A Study in India. New York: New York University Press.

――― (1970b) "Business-government relations become respectable." Columbia J. of World Business (July/August): 27-32.

――― and J. BODDEWYN (forthcoming) International Business-Government Affairs: U. S. Corporate Experience Abroad. New York: American Management Association.

KAPOOR, A. and P. D. GRUB [eds.] (1972) The Multinational Enterprise in Transition. Princeton: Darwin Press.

MODELSKI, G. (1971) "Multinational business: a global perspective." Presented at the meeting of the American Association for the Advancement of Science, December.

PARSONS, T. (1960) Structure and Process in Modern Societies. New York: Free Press.

――― and N. J. SMELSER (1956) Economy and Society. New York: Free Press.

RANDALL, F. F. and J. DUERR (1971) The Public Image of Private Enterprise. New York: Conference Board.

International Oil Companies Confront Governments

A Half-Century of Experience

ROBERT BARNES

Department of Business Administration
York College of Pennsylvania

International business literature regards the company/national government relationship as the crucial problem for analysis. Business leaders know from experience that governments have been both a source of penalties and losses as well as of great profits. Less often observed are the results of systematic investigations of such interactions over long periods—a broader basis for judgments and decision-making. This article highlights the results and implications of such an analysis (Barnes, 1971) for the two traditional leaders of the petroleum industry (Standard Oil Company of New Jersey and the Royal Dutch Shell Group of Companies), covering the period since 1918, and focusing on the problem side of business/government relations. Specifically, an attempt has been made to determine and explain the degree to which this category of world corporations has been able to achieve success in the face of adverse actions by national governments.

Both companies have been leaders in the petroleum industry since its beginning in the latter half of the nineteenth century. The Rockefeller-dominated Standard Oil Trust was created in 1873 and shortly thereafter, established a near monopoly position in the United States in the field of marketing, refining, transportation, and, to a lesser extent, producing oil. In 1899, the Standard Oil Company of New Jersey became the holding company for the Standard Oil interests and has consistently maintained its position as the largest industrial corporation in the world in terms of assets. In 1890, the Royal Dutch Petroleum Company was established through a concession in the Netherlands East Indies; in 1897, the British-owned Shell Transport and Trading Company was established; and in 1907, these two companies merged to form the Royal Dutch Shell Group, which has consistently been the second largest petroleum organization in the world, and the largest industrial group outside the United States in terms of sales, assets, and net profits.

The operations of both companies have, for the most part, been of a similar nature. The Group and "Jersey" have been integrated vertically since 1907 and 1911 respectively (i.e., engaged in all phases of the petroleum business); their production has ranked first in terms of investments followed by manufacturing, marketing, and transportation; both have operated in over 100 countries; the United States has been the principal marketing area for both companies until the late 1960s when the Group reported that most of its net income (54%) and assets (66%) came from Europe and the rest of the Eastern hemisphere; and both companies have had similar histories with respect to geographical sources of supply. The United States was the principal source of production for Jersey until 1932 and for the Group from 1922-1929; and Venezuela has been the principal country of supply for both companies since the 1930s, with the Middle East-North African region becoming predominant in the 1960s (i.e., in 1965, Jersey's Middle Eastern and North African crude oil and natural gas production exceeded that of Venezuela for the first time; and in 1968, Group production in the Middle East was greater than that of Latin America and Canada for the first time).

Relations with Governments

Jersey and the Group have had both unique and similar interactions with governments, although similarities have been most apparent in the more significant producing and marketing countries, especially during the post-World-War-II period. By far the most noteworthy experience for Jersey was the period 1890-1918, the characteristic feature of which was conflict with the U.S. government. The passage of the Sherman Anti-Trust Act in 1890 and the state of Ohio court proceedings in 1892 resulted in dissolution of the Standard Oil Trust Agreement; there were state and federal government suits and fines beginning in 1906 for violation of the Trust Act (i.e., for lessening competition, controlling prices, and deceiving the public); in 1911, a U.S. Supreme Court decision forced Jersey to divest itself of all stock held in 33 of its subsidiaries; and, as late as 1918, the Federal Trade Commission issued a much publicized report which accused oil producers and refineries of profiteering, and stated that if the federal government was to meet its oil requirements, nationalization of the industry might well be necessary. However, cooperation between the company and the government prevailed largely because President Wilson was given sweeping wartime powers and because industry leaders were appointed to key government positions. Company relations with the home government have been a mixture of cooperation and conflict since World War I.

Most of the Group's unique problems have been with the Soviet Union as a result of the 1918 nationalization of the company's petroleum fields; with Romania, beginning in 1919 because of various discriminatory government policies; and in Indonesia during and after World War II. Both companies have had similar difficulties in Mexico, beginning with the 1910-1917 Revolution and ending in the 1938 expropriation; both have seen their holdings in Eastern Europe expropriated in the late 1940s; both have suffered significant tax burdens by Venezuela, the Middle East-North Africa, and the United States beginning in the 1940s; and both companies have had their operations limited by the Suez Crises of 1956 and 1967, by the Iraq expropriation of 1961, and by the nationalization policy of Indonesia beginning in 1965.

Methodology

The method employed for determining whether or to what degree governments have adversely affected company performance consisted of a systematic longitudinal measurement by means of content and statistical analysis of company annual reports for over 50 years. Periodicals and related sources were used to verify the information contained in these reports. The concept of "wealth deprivation" (as opposed to such actions as "expropriation," "nationalism," and so on) was selected in order to provide a more encompassing and sensitive identification of adverse actions which may have been government-related, and which may have had a critical effect on the two companies. Wealth deprivation was defined as any perceived problem which management considered significant enough to mention in their company annual reports, and included such intangibles as threatened congressional investigation as well as taxation and expropriation.

Essentially, three questions were asked in each of the years analyzed since 1918:

(1) Did each company appear to have a satisfactory or successful year?
(2) What was the relative importance and frequency of government- and non-government-related problem categories? and
(3) What was the relative importance and frequency of the various government-related problems?

The tools of analysis for estimating the absolute and relative success of the companies, the relative importance of government, and nongovernment problems, and the nature of these problems consisted of net income, sales, assets, and production levels and growth for the different years; explicit and implicit statements; relative location and space allotted to different factors mentioned in the annual reports; and the frequency with which different problem categories were noted. Direct measurement of the separate and composite government effects on company performance and growth was precluded because of the sheer magnitude of the project and resulting considerations of manageability (i.e., 222 and 311 instances of government-induced deprivations were noted by Jersey and the Group, respectively); lack of sufficient explicit and statistical data; and the inherent difficulty in estimating the costs and effects of the various actions (i.e., expropriations, war, currency manipulations, and so on).

Instead of a direct approach, a series of seven indirect tests was used to help determine whether and the degree to which wealth deprivations affected each company. The first three of the following tests involved the identification and source of company problems, their relative importance over the years, and their relationship to the companies' more significant performance years; while the last four tests analyzed company performance and growth from a number of perspectives:

(1) a comparison of government and nongovernment sources of wealth deprivation in terms of relative importance and frequency;

(2) a "no-problem" analysis of producing and marketing countries;

(3) a comparison of wealth deprivation and relatively significant years in terms of net income loss and gain;

(4) an analysis of satisfactory and possibly satisfactory performance;

(5) a "no-growth" analysis of the four performance indicators of net income, total revenue, total assets, and gross production of crude oil and natural gas including purchases under special contract;

(6) an analysis of performance levels and growth both absolutely and by percentage;

(7) a comparison of company growth with noncompany growth criteria including that of the U.S. petroleum industry, U.S. gross national product, and world production.

Findings—The Nature and Effects of Wealth Deprivation

Table 1 shows government-induced wealth deprivation within a framework of seven interrelated categories, and on the basis of frequency, relative importance, and trends during four time periods. Taxation was seen as the most significant category from the standpoint of relative importance in the post-World-War-II years, the most recent ten-year period, and trends. In terms of actual losses to date from all wealth deprivation

TABLE 1

GOVERNMENT-INDUCED WEALTH DEPRIVATIONS/PROBLEMS
(totals for various periods)

	Expro-priation	War-Related	Indirect Gvt. (Pol)	Other Direct Gvt. (Pol/Ec)	Indirect Gvt. (Ec.)	Tax	Labor
STANDARD OIL COMPANY (New Jersey)							
Frequency[a]							
1918-1945	14	14	3	33	17	18	1
1946-1969	24	12	11	37	10	25	3
1960-1969	20	2	3	12	1	16	0
1918-1969	38	26	14	70	27	43	4
Relative Importance[b]							
1918-1945	3	4	0	14	0	5	0
1946-1969	3	6	3	5	5	8	0
1960-1969	2	2	0	2	0	5	0
1918-1969	6	10	3	17	5	13	0
ROYAL DUTCH SHELL GROUP OF COMPANIES							
Frequency							
1918-1945	17	22	5	75	19	34	10
1946-1969	13	14	20	34	15	31	2
1960-1969	8	5	0	6	2	12	0
1918-1969	30	36	25	109	34	65	12
Relative Importance							
1918-1945	2	10	0	3	9	3	1
1946-1969	0	7	1	2	1	12	0
1960-1969	0	2	0	1	0	7	0
1918-1969	2	17	1	5	10	15	0

SOURCE: Company Annual Reports 1918-1969.
a. Number of instances category was mentioned in company annual reports.
b. Number of years category was considered most important.

categories, it appears that Venezuelan taxation in 1958 was the single most important instance. By far, the largest earnings decline in the history of both companies occurred in that year, when 40% of Jersey's reduction was due to an increase of some $90 million to its tax burden while the Group paid an additional $53 million in Venezuelan income taxes. Expropriation and related actions were at least the second largest source of deprivation for both companies on the basis of individual losses reported (i.e., the depreciated book value of Jersey's 1968 loss in Peru was $85 million, although the actual value of the property was estimated at $170 million). Further, Jersey mentioned this problem more than any other category from 1960-1969, while the Group considered it second only to taxation in terms of frequency during the most recent ten-year period observed. Other important actions noted were those by Indonesia in 1965 and 1969, by Iraq in 1961, by Mexico in 1938, and by the Soviet Union in 1918. War-related problems were second only to taxation in terms of relative importance during the post-World-War-II period for both companies. Principal losses noted were the closing of the Suez Canal and destruction of the Iraq Petroleum Company pipeline system in 1956, which had a significant effect on the above-mentioned earnings losses in 1958 for both companies; and the World War II losses of the Group's operations and assets in the Far East, Europe, Venezuela, and the United States.

The results of most tests for both companies suggest that *the effect of wealth deprivation by governments has not been negative to the point of preventing a satisfactory and improving performance and growth during the past half-century*. The first three tests, which consisted of fourteen separate measurements, resulted in six cases in which the effects of government problems were relatively insignificant (negative), versus five cases where the effects were significant (positive), and three cases which were considered unclear. The four remaining tests, which included seventeen different measurements, revealed ten cases where company performance seemed to improve versus two cases in which there was an opposite finding, and five cases which were unclear.

Both companies perceived government-induced problems as more important than those of nongovernment about half and possibly most of the time (i.e., 58-77% of the time for Royal Dutch Shell and 48-58% for Jersey). Also, while there has been an absolute increase in non-government-related problems, the frequency of government-induced problems has been significantly higher than those of nongovernment throughout the 1918-1969 period.

A comparison of the eighteen most significant years for each company with respect to growth and decline of annual earnings is at least suggestive (see Table 2). For both companies, government problems were dominant in most of the companies' nine best years (i.e., in five to eight of the Group's nine highest growth years versus eight for Jersey).

However, there was less consistency in the worst years since government problems were perceived to be dominant in six to seven of the Group's worst years as compared to only two to four years for Jersey. This partial finding, that whereas a number of earnings losses have been associated with nongovernmental factors, practically all gains have been government-related in nature, would seem to have one or more of the following implications: (1) adverse actions by governments have had no significant effect on the companies; (2) adverse actions by governments have had in some way a positive or stimulating effect on ' the companies; or (3) nongovernmental factors represent the chief source of wealth deprivation, especially in the case of Jersey.

It is interesting to note that the same wealth deprivation categories were dominant in both the nine best and nine worst years for the two companies (i.e., "war," in the case of the Group, and "taxation," for Jersey). A search for trends revealed that both companies' nine highest growth years occurred during the post-World-War-II period at the same time that government problems were becoming relatively more important. However, it should also be noted that the worst year for each company occurred since World War II (in 1958), when government problems were relatively more important, and that these losses were greater than the companies' best earning years.

An analysis of satisfactory and possibly satisfactory performance and growth indicates that both companies apparently experienced good years most of the time (i.e., 75% of the time for Jersey and 69% of the time for the Group). Further, there has been an improving trend, in that Jersey has experienced 20 satisfactory years in the 1946-1969 period versus 17 in the preceding 24 years, while the Group has had 20 satisfactory years in the same post-World-War-II period as compared to only 12 from 1922-1945. It should be noted, however, that there were only 8 years for each company, or about 15% of the time,

TABLE 2
WEALTH DEPRIVATIONS IN RELATIVELY SIGNIFICANT YEARS

	Million U.S. Dollars	Most Important Government-induced Wealth Deprivation	Relative Importance of Government and non-Government Problems
Standard Oil Company (New Jersey)[a]			
1. Relatively Large Annual Net Income Declines			
1958	243	Tax–Venezuela War–Suez Crisis of 1956	Government
1969	34 or 229[c]	Expropriation-Peru	Nongovernment
1921	130	None noted	Nongovernment
1949	96	Currency restrictions	Nongovernment
1930	78	U.S. laws (supply/tariff)	?
1927	77	Tax–Mexico	Nongovernment
1938	72	U.S. conservation laws	Nongovernment
1965	63	Taxes–U.S. and Foreign	?
1942	59	War–U.S., Netherlands East Indies, L.A.	Government
2. Relatively Large Annual Net Income Growth			
1963	178	Tax–General	Government
1950	139	Inflationary policies	Government
1951	132	Expropriation–Iran	Government
1955	124	Taxes–General	Government
1968	122	Expropriation–Peru	Government
1967	101	War–closure of Suez Canal and pipelines	Government
1956	100	Taxes/War (Suez)	Government
1948	97	Dollar exchange shortage in Europe	Government
1947	92	Inflation/War	Nongovernment

	Dollars/ Florins	Most Important Government-induced Wealth Deprivation	Relative Importance of Government and non-Government Problems
Royal Dutch Shell Group of Companies/Royal Dutch Petroleum Company[b]			
1. Relatively Large Annual Net Income Declines			
1958	$185 million	War–Suez Crisis of 1956 Tax–Venezuela	?
1964	$ 13 million	Tax–O.P.E.C. Governments	Nongovernment
1931	63 million Fl.	Monetary Policies-G.B.	Government
1939	62 million Fl.	War	Government
1930	35 million Fl.	Consumption policies–USSR	Government
1921	25 million Fl.	War	Government
1922	16 million Fl.	Exchange rate policies	Nongovernment
1947	6 million Fl.	Taxation–general	Government
1941	3 million Fl.	War	Government
1923	3 million Fl.	Expropriation–USSR	Nongovernment

TABLE 2 (Continued)

	Dollars/ Florins	Most Important Government-induced Wealth Deprivation	Relative Importance of Government and non- Government Problems
2. Relatively Large Annual Net Income Growth			
1968	$133 million	War−Middle East	Government
1957	$ 92 million	War−Middle East	Government
1969	$ 81 million	Tax−U.S.	Nongovernment
1956	$ 71 million	War−Middle East	Government
1967	$ 70 million	War−Middle East	Government
1955	$ 61 million	Tax−General/Venezuela	Government
1962	$ 49 million	Tax−General	?
1959	$ 47 million	Tax−General	?
1965	$ 44 million	Tax−Libya	?

a. Annual Reports of Standard Oil Company (New Jersey), 1918-1969.
b. Annual Reports of Royal Dutch Petroleum Company, 1918-1969.
c. $195 million was for extraordinary charges including $110 million for losses which may be sustained because of certain agricultural chemical and other nonpetroleum losses, and $85 million which represented the depreciated book value of International Petroleum Company property seized by the Peruvian Government. (The actual value was perceived to be more than $170 million.)

when explicit statements and other evidence clearly indicated that satisfactory performance has taken place.

A "growth/no-growth" analysis shows that all four performance indicators of both companies grew during most of the years since 1918 (i.e., 65% of the time for the Group and 54% for Jersey). An analysis of performance levels and growth shows improvement in most cases for both companies (see Table 3). A comparison of the U.S. GNP growth with that of the four performance indicators of the two companies favors the companies in terms of both growth consistency and percentage growth. With regard to company share of world crude oil production since 1926 (the earliest comparable year available), both companies have either maintained or increased their positions, although there has been a slight decline in the most recent years. Jersey increased its world production share from 5.4% in 1926 to 12.6% in 1969 with most of these years above 10%, but with a decline from 14-15% level during most of the 1944-1958 period to a 12-13% level since that time. The Group has managed to maintain its world production share at between 10 and 12% throughout the period (i.e., from 10% in 1926 to

TABLE 3

ABSOLUTE LEVELS AND GROWTH OF PERFORMANCE INDICATORS (1920-1970)

	Total Revenue (Mil.$)	Net Income (Mil.$)	Total Assets (Mil.$)	Gross Production (Barrels/day)
THE STANDARD OIL COMPANY (New Jersey)				
1920 Levels	659	164	1,102	96,451
Growth	723	−122	669	184,549
1930 Levels	1,382	42	1,771	281,000
Growth	−560	82	301	358,889
1940 Levels	822	124	2,071	639,889
Growth	3,354	284	2,116	584,111
1950 Levels	4,176	408	4,188	1,224,000
Growth	4,739	271	5,902	1,290,000
1960 Levels	8,915	689	10,090	2,154,000
Growth	9,782	620	9,152	3,579,000
1970 Levels	18,697	1,309	19,242	6,093,000
The Royal Dutch Shell Group of Companies				
1920 Levels	NA	45	225	NA
Growth	NA	−9	292	NA
1930 Levels	NA	36	517	479,600
Growth	NA	−23	67	NA
1940 Levels	NA	13	584	NA
Growth	NA	129	1,797	NA
1950 Levels	NA	143	2,381	1,245,000
Growth	NA	354	6,520	1,324,000
1960 Levels	7,573	497	8,900	2,569,000
Growth	8,673	383	8,979	3,106,000
1970 Levels	16,246	880	17,879	5,675,000

SOURCE: Annual Company Reports 1920-1970.

10.7% in 1969) with a decline from 12% during the 1950s to 11% during most of the 1960s.

Explanations

The major findings of this study are that, in the period under review, the world's two major international oil companies have been largely invulnerable to governmental actions. Even while exposed to a variety of forms of wealth deprivation, they have flourished, prospered, and grown almost without interruption for half a century. To account for this record of success, we have recourse to two sets of explanations, each focusing on particular characteristic features of these companies—namely, (1) their power, and (2) their EPG profile (that is, the degree to which the companies may be described as ethnocentric, polycentric, or geocentric).

SUCCESS THROUGH POWER?

Five sources of power seem to explain much of the growth and dominance of Jersey and Royal Dutch Shell. First, the power of their home countries. The leading political and economic positions of the home governments provided petroleum and financial resources, markets, and an educational base from which to obtain and maintain a technological and economic lead within the industry. Second, global operations. Because these companies were active in so many countries, government actions in any one country could not critically damage their overall operations. Third, superior technological knowhow in all phases of the oil business, including logistics, refining, and marketing, would appear to explain (at least partially) why the companies have not been forced to terminate operations in the more lucrative countries.

Fourth, successful integration into the world elite structure. There has been evidence of a world elite group of business and government decision makers whose economic interests often transcend sometimes conflicting professional roles, national interests, and cultures of developed and less-developed countries. The continued willingness of succeeding company, Venezuelan, and Middle East/North African government leaders to negotiate suggests a predominating mutual interest and intellectual consensus based on common economic interest. Fifth, successful alliances and cooperation among companies and governments possessing close cultural and economic ties. Examples of this include: cooperation between the two companies in the area of marketing in 1928 (i.e., the famous "As Is" agreement); cooperation among the companies and with the American government in restricting production during the 1930s and in relaxing the anti-trust laws in times of political and economic emergencies; and the Western power alliances which resulted in joint concessions for their companies in the Middle East.

SUCCESS THROUGH GEOCENTRISM?

The other set of notions which could help to explain company success concerns Perlmutter's (1969) concept of "geocentrism." In other words, is this success significantly correlated with company development toward a "geocentric" character as measured on an EPG profile?[1] The results of this preliminary investigation show that, while both companies have had a mixed profile and have shown a number of preconditions for a geocentric attitude, the Group has been decidedly geocentric, whereas Jersey has been equally geocentric and ethnocentric, with a definite movement in the latter direction since 1945.[2]

1. Perlmutter classifies multinational corporations according to three types of headquarters orientations toward subsidiaries as they relate to seven categories of organizational design. The three attitudes are: an ethnocentric (E) or home-country orientation; a polycentric (P) or host-country orientation (i.e., accommodation); and a geocentric (G) or worldwide approach in both headquarters and subsidiaries (i.e., deemphasis of nationalities in favor of the whole). Each company is assigned a score on each of these dimensions, the result being an EPG profile.

2. Of the 36 EPG characteristics noted for Jersey, 4 were polycentric, 15 ethnocentric, and 17 geocentric, although 11 of the latter occurred before 1951. Of the 19 EPG traits noted for the Group, 4 were polycentric, 4 ethnocentric, and 11 geocentric with no trends observed.

The difference in profiles is most clearly seen in the areas of ownership, management, and policies-philosophies of the two companies. The broader binational ownership and distribution of Group shares among five different European-North Atlantic nationalities suggests a higher degree of geocentrism.[3] The same orientation is observed with respect to middle- and upper-management levels in that the Group has done the most in placing different nationalities in the Hague and London headquarters staffs; and in developing chief executive officers of foreign affiliates and interchanging them regardless of nationality. Jersey, on the other hand, has displayed a more polycentric tendency by developing employees for higher positions in their respective countries. A review of the companies' top management decision makers indicates that the typical background of Jersey executives has continued to be inbred and confined to the Western hemispheres (ethnocentric). In contrast, John Loudon, the former chairman of the Group's Committee of Managing Directors and member of a family which has held controlling positions since 1902, is a nephew of a foreign minister, son of a diplomat, possesses equal fluency in the thinking and mores of many nations, speaks five languages fluently, and has stated that one cannot afford to take a narrow national viewpoint. Also, the Group has been consistently cooperative (polycentric) in its policy statements concerning governments over the years, while, in the case of Jersey, there has been a conspicuous absence in this type of philosophy in favor of remarks which are more "hard-line" and critical, especially of host governments (ethnocentric or geocentric).

The organizations of both companies have displayed both centralized and decentralized tendencies (i.e., ethnocentrism and polycentrism respectively). Jersey has taken significant

3. The Royal Dutch Petroleum Company and the Shell Transport and Trading Company, Ltd. are the parent companies for the Royal Dutch Shell Group of companies, and have a 60-40% share of interest respectively in the Group. A recent estimate of the proportion in which the shares of the combined parent companies are held in the various countries are: United Kingdom—39%, United States—19%, Netherlands—18%, France—14%, Switzerland—9%, and Others—1%. The Standard Oil Company (N.J.) is primarily American-oriented in terms of ownership and control, since 99% of its shareholders live in the United States.

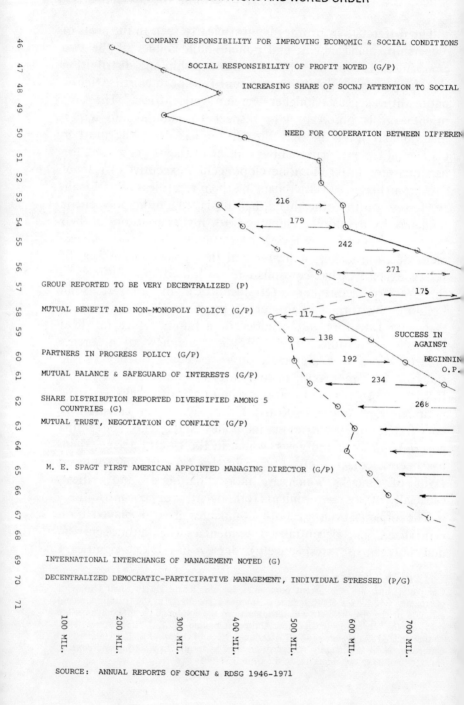

COMPANY RESPONSIBILITY FOR IMPROVING ECONOMIC & SOCIAL CONDITIONS

SOCIAL RESPONSIBILITY OF PROFIT NOTED (G/P)

INCREASING SHARE OF SOCNJ ATTENTION TO SOCIAL

NEED FOR COOPERATION BETWEEN DIFFEREN

216

179

242

271

175

GROUP REPORTED TO BE VERY DECENTRALIZED (P)

MUTUAL BENEFIT AND NON-MONOPOLY POLICY (G/P)   117

138   SUCCESS IN
                                                               AGAINST
PARTNERS IN PROGRESS POLICY (G/P)   192   BEGINNIN
                                                              O.P.
MUTUAL BALANCE & SAFEGUARD OF INTERESTS (G/P)
                                                     234
SHARE DISTRIBUTION REPORTED DIVERSIFIED AMONG 5   268
    COUNTRIES (G)
MUTUAL TRUST, NEGOTIATION OF CONFLICT (G/P)

M. E. SPAGT FIRST AMERICAN APPOINTED MANAGING DIRECTOR (G/P)

INTERNATIONAL INTERCHANGE OF MANAGEMENT NOTED (G)

DECENTRALIZED DEMOCRATIC-PARTICIPATIVE MANAGEMENT, INDIVIDUAL STRESSED (P/G)

100 MIL.   200 MIL.   300 MIL.   400 MIL.   500 MIL.   600 MIL.   700 MIL.

SOURCE: ANNUAL REPORTS OF SOCNJ & RDSG 1946-1971

Figure 1: COMPANY GROWTH AND EGP PROFILE, 1946-1971 (STANDARD OIL CO. OF N.J. AND ROYAL DUTCH SHELL) IN MILLIONS OF U.S. DOLLARS

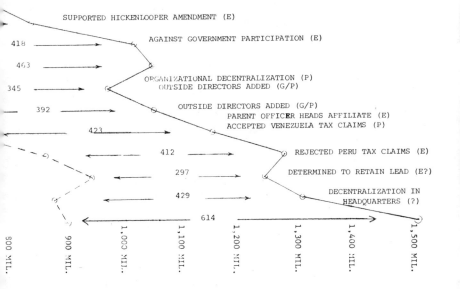

G/P)

PROBLEMS (G/P)

NATIONALITIES AND FAIR PARTICIPATION OF BENEFITS (G/P)

NOTE: _____ SOCNJ NET EARNINGS
       -----RDSG NET EARNINGS
       (G) GEOCENTRISM
       (P) POLYCENTRISM
       (E) ETHNOCENTRISM

99% OF SHAREHOLDERS U.S. (E)

AGAINST INCREASED GOVERNMENT CONTROL (E?)

LOPING HOST COUNTRY MANAGEMENT (P)
REASED GOVERNMENT CONTROL (E?)
    DECENTRALIZATION (P)
    FORMED IN REACTION TO ALLEGED SOCNJ PRICE ACTION (E)

SUPPORTED HICKENLOOPER AMENDMENT (E)

AGAINST GOVERNMENT PARTICIPATION (E)

418

463

345   ORGANIZATIONAL DECENTRALIZATION (P)
           OUTSIDE DIRECTORS ADDED (G/P)

    392   OUTSIDE DIRECTORS ADDED (G/P)
                 PARENT OFFICER HEADS AFFILIATE (E)
                 ACCEPTED VENEZUELA TAX CLAIMS (P)

        423

          412   REJECTED PERU TAX CLAIMS (E)

          297   DETERMINED TO RETAIN LEAD (E?)

          429   DECENTRALIZATION IN
                             HEADQUARTERS (?)

              614

800 MIL.   900 MIL.   1,000 MIL.   1,100 MIL.   1,200 MIL.   1,300 MIL.   1,400 MIL.   1,500 MIL.

steps toward decentralization in 1927, when it ceased to be both a holding and operating company, in 1965 when it delegated certain functions to regional organizations, and in 1966 when it appointed to its board two outside directors. At the same time, the company has been characterized as remarkably centralized by 1960; and the appointment of a parent company officer to head its largest subsidiary (Humble Oil Company) in 1965 rather than continuing the tradition of promotion from within, was seen as a step backward toward centralization. In contrast, there have been no such moves toward decentralization by the seven managing directors of the Group, except that its principal affiliate, the Shell Oil Company in the United States, has reportedly been characterized as having extensive autonomy, and thus may be more decentralized than in the case of Jersey.

The operations of both companies have tended to become more geocentric because of the growing number of significant producing and consuming countries. However, Jersey has maintained more of a home-country (ethnocentric) orientation because of the relative importance of the United States as a petroleum source and market, which has at the same time placed the Group in a host-country (polycentric) role. From another perspective, it seems plausible that both companies' actions have been selectively polycentric, since only in the relatively significant producing and consuming countries has there been sufficient cooperation and compromise to prevent termination of company operations by host governments.

The implications from these EPG findings are several. First, the various steps which both companies have taken in the direction of geocentrism may have contributed toward the necessary amount of cooperation and compromise with governments around the world to permit success. However, because there are certain dimensions of geocentrism which are still lacking in both companies (i.e., Jersey's management, ownership, and policies; the Group's Board of Directors' structure; or both companies' organization, operations, and government relations), the net effect of these companies' actions has been unclear. Another implication is that, since neither company has been purely geocentric in most of the six areas observed, and since Jersey has been less geocentric of the two companies while maintaining a slightly better performance and growth (see Tables 3 and 4), then perhaps geocentrism is not the primary explanatory variable. It should be noted that the most distinct association has been that of earnings and movements toward decentralization (polycentrism) by Jersey in 1927 and 1965. Both actions occurred during a period of earnings declines and were immediately followed by at least two years of earnings growth.

Conclusions

These explanatory findings are no more than tentative. In its relations with governments, company power has been important, but its importance may have been declining somewhat in recent years in the face of increasing resistance and hostility. This, in turn, may have been stimulated by the inherent instability of a balance of power system as well as by certain ethnocentric tendencies of business and even governments. However, because of indications that both companies may have been primarily polycentric in significant areas, this analysis should be sensitive to the possibility that the more accommodating attitude of polycentrism has indeed been more closely associated with company growth and success than has that of geocentrism. Although these tentative findings in this complex interdisciplinary field leave many questions unanswered and calling for more research, they do suggest at least partial evidence for those who need to speculate about the outcome of future encounters between governments and large oil companies.

REFERENCES

BARNES, R. G. (1971) "World corporations and wealth deprivations by governments: a partial and exploratory analysis of the experiences of Standard Oil Company (N.J.) and the Royal Dutch Shell Group of companies." Ph.D. dissertation. University of Washington.

PERLMUTTER, H. V. (1969) "The tortuous evolution of the multinational corporation." Columbia J. of World Business (January/February): 9-18.

Elite Attitudes Toward Multinational Firms

A Study of Britain, Canada, and France

JOHN FAYERWEATHER

Graduate School of Business Administration
New York University

The future evolution of multinational firms will depend to a large degree on the policy decisions of host nations, made essentially by leadership groups. Thus, knowledge of how elites feel about foreign business firms is a key element in analysis of the outlook for international business.

There have been assorted expressions of elite attitudes on multinational firms including official national policies, speeches, and popular writing. But there have been no studies to identify systematically the views of the significant elite groups. To fill this gap, I undertook surveys in Britain and France in late 1970 and Canada in late 1971, results of which are summarized in this article.

The Surveys

The surveys covered four groups—national legislators, permanent government officials, heads of business firms, and labor

AUTHOR'S NOTE: I am indebted to my colleague, Professor Jean Boddewyn, for help in formulating the questionnaire and preparing the French translation and to my research assistants, Richard Sorrenson and Peter Sugges, for computer analysis of the data. Experts in Britain, Canada, and France too numerous to list provided invaluable advice and help in the survey.

union leaders. A mail questionnaire was employed for reasons of breadth of coverage, economy, objectivity, and anonymity, the latter point applying especially to the government officials. For each group in each country, about 200 questionnaires were mailed.

Mail surveys of foreign elites, especially government and labor groups, are not common, and they present assorted problems. This study provided a variety of useful insights on methodology for such surveys, but space permits noting only a few highlights here. More details will be set forth in later writings. It was assumed that a major handicap to be overcome was the image of a meddling American question asker with little interest in the welfare of the host country. The author has devoted substantial time to seeing problems from the host country viewpoint by frequent communication with host nationals, most recently during residence in France in the fall of 1970 and assorted trips to Canada in 1971. A strong effort was made to convey an image along these lines in the cover letter. With appropriate permission, the author noted in the letter that he had sought advice from specific organizations in each country (e.g., the Canadian Institute of International Affairs and the Private Planning Association of Canada). Also, French and Canadian return addresses were used.

While it is difficult to judge the effect of these and other efforts to encourage response, they apparently had a positive result. Some competent advisers were quite doubtful about the prospects of adequate response, especially with some groups like the French *fonctionnaires* who are notably suspicious of *investigateurs*. But the methodology, supported undoubtedly by the strong interest in the subject matter, proved satisfactory. A response of about 25% had been expected, giving a statistically satisfactory group of 50 replies per group. In fact the response rates were generally well in excess of this minimum:

	Legislators	Government officials	Business heads	Labor leaders
Britain	30%	29%	25%	41%
Canada	23%	40%	30%	30%
France	26%	39%	25%	47%

Essentially, the same questionnaire was used in all countries. The standard translation and retranslation process was applied for the version used for the French and French-Canadians. A question on labor union recognition had to be changed because of legal differences in the countries; one question was rephrased for Canada because of unsatisfactory results in the European surveys; three questions were dropped and one added for Canada. Much of the information sought in the questions applies to the author's long-term studies of the relation of nationalism to multinational firms. Only the main responses bearing on the expressed attitudes of the elites are reported in this article.

The questionnaire provided for responses on a 7-point scale. The right-left location of response options was varied in an erratic manner to avoid repetitive answers. In the data in this article, the responses have been reversed where appropriate, so that 1 always indicates the most favorable attitude toward foreign firms and 7, the least favorable. Except as noted, the data are mean scores for groups. The tables also show averages of mean scores for the four groups for each country. These averages of averages are questionable in statistical methodology but are a convenience for readers in putting the data in perspective. In order to devote maximum space to reporting results, comments are not made about statistical significance for each table. Significance values differ from question to question because of differences in number of answers and standard deviations. However, as a general rule of thumb, the reader may assume that differences of 0.7 are always significant at the .005 level. Those from 0.4 to 0.6 are sometimes significant. Those below 0.4 are rarely so.

The Subject in Perspective

To place the opinions of the leaders in overall perspective, two broad questions were asked at the outset of the questionnaire: (A) how great an effect the operations of foreign

TABLE 1
OVERALL OPINIONS

Q.A — How great an affect do you believe the operations of foreign companies in X have on X?   Small = 1;   Large = 7.

Q.B — In your opinion what is the overall effect on X of the activities of foreign companies in X?   Good = 1;   Bad = 7

For "X" in all questions read "Great Britain" (British); "France" (French) or "Canada" (Canadian)

		Leg	PG	Lab	Bus	Ave
Q.A. —	Br.	5.0	5.0	5.2	4.4	4.9
	Fr.	4.5	4.9	4.9	3.9	4.6
	Can.	5.6	6.1	6.3	5.9	6.0
Q.B. —	Br.	3.2	2.8	4.0	2.9	3.2
	Fr.	3.1	3.1	4.3	2.8	3.3
	Can.	3.5	3.2	4.2	2.6	3.4

Leg = National legislators; PG = Permanent government officials; Lab = Labor union leaders; and Bus = Heads of business firms

companies had on their country, and (B) whether the overall effect was good or bad. The results are shown in Table 1.

The responses to question A indicate that most of the leaders regard the impact of foreign investment in their country as a matter of substantial magnitude with scores ranging from 4.4 to 6.3 along a scale from 1 = small to 7 = large. As might be expected, the Canadian scores are distinctly higher. With 60% of their manufacturing industry foreign-controlled vs. around 10% for the British and the French, there is a major difference. If the data hold any surprise, it is that the European and Canadian scores do not differ more.

Question B reveals a moderate overall favorable appraisal by most groups, with scores around 3 (4 would be neutral). Thus, despite a number of negative reactions on specific points which will be noted later, the majority of the leaders seem solidly favorable in their judgment of the net effect of the role of multinational firms in their countries. The other significant feature is the substantial similarity across countries among the groups: the businessmen, except in Britain, are the most favorable; the two government groups are close to them; and

TABLE 2

CRITERIA FOR EVALUATING FOREIGN FIRMS:
Computed Rank Order Scores, 1 = Most Important

	Britain					France					Canada				
	Leg	PG	Lab	Bus	Ave	Leg	PG	Lab	Bus	Ave	Leg	PG	Lab	Bus	Ave
Effect on X national income	1.0	1.0	1.0	1.0	1.0	1.0	1.0	1.1	1.0	1.0	1.5	1.4	1.0	1.2	1.3
	(2.2)	(2.3)	(2.1)	(2.8)		(2.5)	(2.5)	(2.1)	(2.4)		(2.9)	(2.4)	(2.0)	(2.6)	
Effect on balance of payments	1.0	1.0	1.1	1.1	1.1	1.3	1.3	1.1	1.4	1.3	1.1	1.6	1.8	1.1	1.4
Control over national affairs	1.4	1.7	1.6	1.3	1.5	1.2	1.0	1.1	1.5	1.2	1.0	1.0	1.1	1.2	1.1
Benefits for X workers	1.1	2.0	1.0	1.1	1.3	1.3	1.6	1.0	1.9	1.4	1.8	1.6	1.0	1.3	1.4
Opportunities for X managers	1.8	2.4	2.0	1.6	2.0	2.1	3.0	2.7	2.1	2.2	1.5	1.9	1.9	1.0	1.6
Role of X in the world	1.8	2.8	2.1	1.3	2.0	1.1	1.5	1.6	1.7	1.5	1.5	1.4	1.0	1.2	1.3
Changes in X way of life	2.4	3.0	2.6	2.4	2.6	1.8	2.0	2.0	2.1	2.0	2.1	2.3	2.2	2.4	2.2
Opportunities for X investors	3.1	3.4	2.9	2.0	2.8	2.7	3.6	3.2	1.8	2.8	2.1	2.1	1.9	1.2	1.8

X = British, French or Canadian

BASIS. Question "How important should the following considerations be in judging the value of foreign companies operating in X?"
Major Importance = 1; Minor = 7.

NOTE: In the above table the consideration with the lowest average score for each group was given the rank of 1.0. The ranks of the other criteria are the sum of 1.0 plus the difference between their scores and those of the top ranked criteria for the group, e.g. for British MP's. Effects on National Income had an actual score of 2.2 and Opportunities for Investors, 4.3. The actual average scores of first item are given in parentheses.

the labor leaders are clearly set apart, with a slightly adverse judgment.[1]

CRITERIA FOR EVALUATING FOREIGN FIRMS

Table 2 gives a picture of the criteria by which the merits of foreign firms are judged. The respondents were asked to rate the importance of eight criteria on the scale from major (1) to minor (7). The table is designed to show the most significant facts—the rank and relative weight of each criterion. The criterion rated as most important by each group is given a rank of 1.0. The rank numbers of the other criteria indicate the difference between their actual scores and those of the top-ranked criteria.

A variety of features appear on Table 2. Most obvious is the consistent prominence of the top three criteria. With a few exceptions, economic and control considerations rank close to the top of all lists. There is little statistically significant distinction among the scores of these three in most cases. However, the pattern of differences among countries is interesting. The effects of foreign investment on control of national affairs seem to loom somewhat larger in the eyes of Canadians than of Europeans. A notable feature is the generally much lower ranking of effects on the national way of life by all elites. It appears that, at least among leadership groups, the highly publicized reaction against the "Americanization" of Canada

1. An obvious question in this whole survey is the possible bias of those who responded as compared with nonrespondents. A full check on this point was not feasible, but a check was made of one group. A random sample of 20% of the Canadian Members of Parliament was covered directly by a researcher. (The interviewing was done by Bruce Thordarson with guidance from Julian Payne of the Canadian Parliamentary Centre in Ottawa.) They were asked whether they had returned the questionnaire, and they each answered question B on Table 1. Some 30% had responded, compared to the 24% rate for all MP's surveyed. The average of the scores of the nonrespondents on question B was 2.3 and for the respondents it was 3.0 compared to 3.5 for MP's responding to the mail questionnaire. These latter figures indicate that the group was either not comparable to the mail respondents or that the direct checking process elicited different responses. However, the main point is the apparent favorable bias among nonrespondents. One cannot with assurance assume a bias of similar magnitude or direction among other groups, but it is at least a fair possibility. Thus, the indications of favorable overall attitudes from the mail survey are reinforced.

and Europe is of distinctly less importance than economic and political effects.

Among the effects on specific national groups, the labor element stands out as definitely most significant. The highest rating for it naturally comes from the union leaders, but there is substantial reinforcing support from other groups. The chief deviation from this pattern is the high ranking of opportunities for both managers and investors in Canada by businessmen. It seems likely that this is a product of the relatively large scale of foreign investment in Canada. If only 10% of manufacturing firms are foreign-owned, local investors and managers presumably feel little effect on their opportunities, but at 60% or so, the impact is of real concern.

The rankings for the role of the nation in the world may reflect this same sort of reaction. The Canadians generally place this criterion appreciably higher than do the Europeans. One may surmise that the massive impact of U.S. investment makes the Canadians more concerned about its effect on the whole character of their nation. The other score that strikes one in this criterion is the 1.1 for French legislators. One gathers that, among deputies, General de Gaulle's preoccupation with the glory of France struck a sympathetic chord.

Another interesting way to look at Table 2 is to compare the spread of scores. For British and French business leaders and all Canadian groups, the spreads are 1.4 or less, while for other British and French groups they tend to be appreciably higher, 1.7 up to 2.6. Doubtless, a number of factors are at work here, but two suggest themselves as possible explanations. First, among the Europeans, it is likely that rather specialized interests and responsibilities of government and labor people lead to discrimination as to the importance of criteria, whereas the businessmen have a more diffused picture which results in less discrimination among effects of foreign investment. The Canadian story, on the other hand, may be one more manifestation of the difference between foreign investment on a major versus a minor scale. The massive impact of foreign firms in Canada elevates all sorts of effects to prominence in the eyes of varied groups.

Performance Appraisal

Most of the questions in the survey were designed to elicit attitudes on effects of foreign firms on four aspects of host nation affairs: economics, control, culture, and labor. The results of these questions will be considered separately and in relation to each other.

ECONOMIC IMPACT

The three questions in Table 3 are different ways of looking at the economic impact of foreign firms. Question C suggests a rather broad appraisal of economic contribution. Among British and French elites, with the exception of the union leaders, the appraisals here are moderately but clearly favorable. In Canada, the weight of opinion is on the other side: all except the business leaders take a negative view. This is an interesting judgment, somewhat at variance with the view commonly heard in Canada that foreign investment has been a good thing for the

TABLE 3

ECONOMIC MEASURES

Q.C — What do you believe is the net economic result of the operations of foreign companies in X? They give more than they take = 1; They take more than they give = 7

Q.D — In relation to their economic contributions, the dividends, royalties, and other payments which foreign companies received from their operations in X are: Too small = 1; Too large = 7

Q.E — Do you feel that the magnitude of the receipts (dividends, royalties, etc.) from X overseas operations in relation to their contributions is: Too small = 1; Too large = 7

		Leg	PG	Lab	Bus	Ave
Q.C	Br.	3.8	3.2	4.8	3.4	3.8
	Fr.	4.1	3.8	5.2	3.3	4.1
	Can.	4.6	4.2	5.2	3.8	4.4
Q.D.	Br.	4.5	4.4	4.9	4.3	4.5
	Fr.	4.5	4.5	5.3	4.2	4.6
	Can.	4.7	4.8	5.6	4.5	4.9
Q.E.	Br.	3.4	3.7	4.2	3.3	3.7
	Fr.	3.5	4.0	4.4	3.6	3.9
	Can.	3.8	4.0	4.0	3.7	3.9

country economically. This view and the responses to question C are not inconsistent, for one can interpret the latter to mean "While we may benefit economically from foreign investment, the foreign firms gain even more." But the implication nonetheless is that, compared with the Europeans, Canadian leaders are skeptical about the balance of economic gains.

Question D is essentially an appraisal of the items which enter into the balance of payments. Here the elites take a distinctly more negative view. In effect, the data say that the balance of external economic benefits and costs is considered clearly adverse to the host country, as compared to the more favorable views on overall economic impact. Another feature of these data is the smaller spread in the average scores among the groups—0.6, 1.1, and 1.1 on question D versus 1.6, 1.9, and 1.4 on question C.

The differences in responses to questions C and D fit a frequently observed picture of opinions about foreign investment. The internal economic benefits from employment gains and inputs of capital and skills are quite widely recognized, though there are substantial differences in the degree of recognition among groups because of differences in impact on specific interests. Consideration of the external balance of costs and benefits, however, brings into play a different type of thinking on which there is more homogeneity among groups. This thinking apparently incorporates elements of both mercantilistic economics and nationalistic defensive reaction against the drain on national wealth by outsiders.

The responses to question E give some further confirmation to the nationalist element in the economic appraisals. This question was one of a small set at the end of the questionnaire in which the respondents were asked to look at the effects of companies from their own nation in other countries. The questions were mirror images of those asked earlier in the questionnaire. In all cases, the average scores on question E are distinctly lower than for question D, the differences ranging from 0.5 to 1.6. If the replies to the two questions were based solely on general economic concepts, there should be no difference in them. That is to say, it is hard to conceive some logic which would demonstrate that the receipts of French companies from subsidiaries in Brazil, India, and the like were more equitably related to their economic inputs than were the payments by subsidiaries in France to parent firms in Germany, the United States, and so on. When we find such a position endorsed across the board by all twelve elite groups, therefore, we must assume that something other than logic is at work. The explanation presumably lies in the nationalistic bias of the respondent considering his nation's interest in the benefits received from investments in other countries in question E as compared to his protective nationalistic reaction against the external drain caused by outside investment in his native country in question D.

THE CONTROL DIMENSION

Tables 4 and 5 describe various ways the elites feel about the effects of foreign companies on control of national affairs. The main dimensions of the picture are expectable and quickly stated. The loss of control is seen as a significant problem (somewhere between major and minor in Table 4, question F) with the impact of American companies a matter of notably greater concern than that of other firms. Furthermore the effects, if greater control is acquired, are quite worrisome (Table 5, question H).

Underlying these attitudes are beliefs that, when companies are foreign-owned, their decisions are more often adverse to national interests than if they are domestically owned (Table 5, question I) and that the home country loyalty of foreign managers creates a moderate problem (question J). The interesting features of the data lie in more refined analysis. They show one really surprising finding and some other intriguing points.

The major surprise is the score for Canada on question F, Table 4. In light of the recent strong public reaction against American control of Canadian industry and the traditional

TABLE 4
CONTROL EFFECTS RELATED TO COUNTRIES

Q.F — To what degree do you feel that the activities of the companies of the following nationalities cause a loss of X control over X affairs? Minor loss of control = 1; Major loss of control = 7

Q.G — What effect do you believe the operations of X companies have on the control of national affairs by the nations of the following countries? Loss of control Minor = 1; Major = 7

(Averages of all elite groups)

Country – Y	Question F - Companies of country Y in X		Question G - X companies in country Y
United States	Br.	4.5	1.8
	Fr.	5.4	1.6
	Can.	4.8	0.9
France	Br.	2.6	2.1
	Can.	2.9	0.7
Britain	Fr.	3.5	2.2
	Can.	3.1	0.8
Canada	Br.		2.5
	Fr.		2.3
Germany	Br.	2.7	
	Fr.	4.3	
	Can.	2.9	
Holland	Br.	2.8	
	Fr.	3.5	
Japan	Br.	2.6	1.8
	Fr.	2.9	1.6
	Can.	3.3	0.8
Brazil	Br.		2.6
	Fr.		2.8

worries in Canada about domination by the "friendly giant" to the south, one would have expected a much stronger adverse score here than for Britain and France—something like 6.0, for example, compared to the 4.5 and 5.4 for the British and French. But no, the Canadians come in with a relatively mild 4.8. As the data in Table 6 show, this pattern holds for all groups. There is actually an indication of greater national consensus in the smaller spread between groups than for the other two countries (0.9 versus 1.2 and 1.5).

There is no apparent simple explanation for this Canadian response. As we saw in Table 2, the control question is as important for Canadians as for the other elites. The Canadian

TABLE 5
CONTROL

Q.H – What will be the result for X if foreign companies have greater control over policy decisions in X industry? Good = 1; Bad = 7

Q.I – How often do you think a typical foreign company operating in X acts in ways contrary to X national interests as compared to a typical X firm? No difference = 1; Frequently = 7

Q.J – How frequently do you believe X firms operating abroad act in ways contrary to the national interests of host countries as compared to a typical local firm? No difference = 1; Frequently = 7

Q.K – To what degree does the loyalty of a foreign manager in X to his own country have a bad effect for X? Minor problem = 1; Major problem = 7

		Leg	PG	Lab	Bus	Ave
Q.H.	– Br.	5.3	4.6	6.0	5.0	5.2
	Fr.	4.8	5.0	5.8	5.1	5.2
	Can.	6.0	5.8	6.3	5.3	5.8
Q.I.	– Br.	3.5	3.0	4.1	3.1	3.4
	Fr.	3.7	4.0	4.3	3.0	3.8
	Can.	3.5	3.8	4.0	3.3	3.6
Q.J.	– Br.	3.2	3.1	3.8	2.4	3.1
	Fr.	3.1	3.5	4.1	2.4	3.3
	Can.	2.7	3.1	3.4	2.7	3.0
Q.K.	– Br.	3.2	2.6	3.8	2.8	3.1
	Fr.	3.7	3.8	4.7	3.2	3.8
	Can.	4.0	3.8	4.3	3.5	3.9

reactions to control by companies of other countries (e.g., Germany and Japan) are sufficiently within the range of those of the British and French so that one cannot say that there has been a general pattern of lower scoring among Canadians for this whole question. The responses to question H indicate that the Canadians do demonstrate a different degree of concern about *future* loss of control. But there is quite solid evidence here that, despite all the public uproar, Canadian elites do not

TABLE 6
LOSS OF CONTROL OF NATIONAL AFFAIRS BECAUSE OF
U.S. COMPANIES (see Question F, Table 4)

	Leg	P G	Lab	Bus	Ave
Britain	4.4	3.9	5.4	4.1	4.5
France	5.1	5.6	6.1	4.9	5.4
Canada	4.5	4.9	5.4	4.5	4.8

in fact look upon the *actual* loss of control resulting from having 60% of their factories foreign-owned as any more of a problem than the British, with less than a tenth of the actual degree of loss of control.

How can one explain this Canadian response? For a conservative researcher, the sound answer must be that it is a puzzling matter to which further research must be directed. But one can advance a few thoughts to which other responses in this survey contribute. The most obvious point is that, in terms of overall national welfare, the elites register a quite consistent and generally favorable appraisal (Table 1, question A). Thus it would appear likely that the reaction on the control question is influenced heavily by political psychology, the importance to national independence of control for itself, more than because of tangible results of that control. If this is so, scores may be expected to be influenced more by the character of nationalism in a country than by the actual amount of foreign investment. The reactions to American control are consistent with this line of reasoning in terms of the general character of nationalism in the three countries. The high French score fits with the French preoccupation with retention of political independence vis-à-vis the United States, the EEC, and so on. An interesting confirmation of this preoccupation appears in the difference in degree of concern over control effects of German firms compared to the British score (4.3 versus 2.7, question F, Table 4). The British, even though they have a greater volume of U.S. investment, are less worried about political control. The Canadians, while vocally expressing concern about political identity, in fact are for the most part hard-headed and pragmatic in acceptance of the realities of political interdependence and powerful influence from the United States. These are, it must be emphasized, tentative explanatory thoughts, but they would seem to provide fruitful hypotheses for further work.

The influence of nationalist attitudes also shows up again in the mirror-image question on control. The responses to questions I and J in Table 5 are similar to those to questions D and

E in Table 3 on economic effects, in that the host elites express a more adverse view of the effects of foreign firms within their own countries than within other countries on identical propositions. One notes, however, an intriguing difference in the degree of bias—score differences of 1.2, 0.7, and 0.7 on the economic question versus 0.3, 0.4, and 0.8 on control. While the pattern is not consistent, there is an apparent tendency toward less bias on the control aspects.

A more complicated but presumably even sounder piece of evidence on the same tack is the scoring of the elites in evaluating the loss of control concerning investment in their own countries (question G, Table 4). Here we have two viewpoints on two factual, identical situations. When British elites consider the activities of French companies in Britain, they score the loss of control at 2.6. When the French elite consider these same activities in Britain, they rate the loss of control slightly lower at 2.2. As to the activities of British firms in France, the French rate the loss at 3.5 and the British, much less serious at 2.1.

The details of these differences may involve a complexity of explanation. But, for present purposes, the obvious point is that, in both cases, there is clearly a tendency to see the loss of control as more serious when it is in your own country embodied in foreign entities than when it is a distant problem in which the potential danger sources are your own nationals. These, of course, are just small pieces of evidence in a complex story, but they give credence to the hypothesis that the worry over loss of control of national affairs springs not only from tangible issues but from a deep-seated reaction to foreign pressure in the host society.

CULTURAL IMPACT

From the data in Table 2, we already know that the elites do not attach major importance to the cultural impact of foreign investment. Table 7 gives other dimensions of their views on this impact.

The elites apparently recognize that a moderate degree of change in national life is induced by the activities of the firms (question L) with the British on the low side (3.3) and the Canadians the high side (4.1). The appraisals of the merits of the effects are all at least slightly favorable, with the one exception of the French union leaders (question M). The even more favorable reaction to management practices of foreign firms (question N) is not unexpected in light of the general respect with which American management is regarded. But the receptivity to foreign ways in personal activities (question O) is stronger than one might have anticipated. Perhaps the most decisive demonstration of the weakness of resistance to cultural penetration is the fact that the proud French have the lowest scores on question O, and that among them, the *hautes fonctionnaires,* the mandarins of their society, along with the

TABLE 7
CULTURAL EFFECTS

Q.L — To what degree do you believe that the influence of foreign ways of life brought in by foreign companies in X changes the X way of life? Small change = 1; Large change = 7

Q.M — Are the changes in way of life referred to in Question (L) good or bad? Good = 1; Bad = 7

Q.N — The general effect on X of changes in methods of management caused by introduction of practices of foreign companies is: Desirable = 1; Undesirable = 7

Q.O — In your personal activities, to what degree do you feel it is desirable to adopt ways of life or work brought in by foreign companies? Large degree = 1; Not at all = 7

		Leg	P G	Lab	Bus	Ave
Q.L —	Br.	3.5	3.2	3.3	3.2	3.3
	Fr.	3.6	4.5	3.6	3.7	3.8
	Can.	4.3	4.0	4.5	3.7	4.1
Q.M —	Br.	3.3	3.8	3.9	3.7	3.7
	Fr.	3.2	3.4	4.3	3.1	3.5
	Can.	3.7	3.9	3.9	3.2	3.7
Q.N —	Br.	2.9	2.7	4.2	2.6	3.1
	Fr.	2.7	2.6	4.1	2.4	2.9
	Can.	3.3	2.8	3.9	2.6	3.2
Q.O —	Br.	4.5	5.3	4.8	4.7	4.7
	Fr.	3.7	3.4	4.6	3.3	3.8
	Can.	4.9	4.8	4.7	4.6	4.8

French businessmen, are the most receptive of all. While these assorted pieces of evidence do not eliminate cultural impact as an issue, they clearly suggest that it is a much lesser one than the economic and control effects of foreign firms.

LABOR RELATIONS

The data in Table 8 indicate some distinct differences in the image of various aspects of the labor relations of foreign firms. The responses to question P affirm the generally observed view that foreign firms pay higher wages than local firms, a point which may at least in the case of Britain not be entirely accurate according to a recent study (Gennard, 1972: 30). When it comes to other working conditions like job security and handling of grievances (question Q), however, the weight of opinion shifts toward a less favorable image overall and a distinctly negative one with the British and French union leaders.

On the third point, union relations, the results present a quite mixed picture. While the questions are not quite comparable,

TABLE 8

LABOR RELATIONS

How do you believe the treatment of workers by foreign companies in X compares with that by X firms in respect to wages and other working conditions (job security, handling of grievances, etc.)?

Q.P — Wages: Foreign firms Better = 1; Worse = 7

Q.Q — Other Conditions: Better = 1; Worse = 7

Q.R — Do you believe that foreign companies in X are more *or* less willing to recognize trade unions than X firms are? (Fr. Q - Disposees . . . a s'entendre avec les syndicats) More willing = 1; Less willing = 7

		Leg	*P G*	*Lab*	*Bus*	*Ave*
Q.P	— Br.	2.6	3.3	3.5	2.8	3.1
	Fr.	2.9	2.7	3.2	3.1	3.0
	Can.	3.3	3.4	3.3	3.3	3.3
Q.Q	— Br.	3.5	3.8	4.5	3.6	3.8
	Fr.	3.8	3.5	4.8	3.8	4.0
	Can.	3.7	3.8	3.6	3.5	3.6
Q.R	— Br.	4.9	4.3	5.6	4.3	4.7
	Fr.	3.8	3.6	5.0	4.0	4.1
	Can.	3.3	3.4	3.4	3.1	3.3

the data confirm a general impression that in France there is not the same intensity of struggle between unions and foreign firms as in Britain. In Canada, the situation is clearly quite different. It is notable that not only are the scores generally lower, but that the union leaders themselves rate the foreign firms as more tractable than domestic companies.

THE "JOINT-VENTURE SYNDROME"

From Japan to Canada to Chile, the most popular host nation desire seems to be that multinational firms subordinate their role by investing in local enterprises on a minority ownership basis. A set of six questions in the survey was designed to shed some light on elite attitudes on this subject. The respondents were asked to rate the effects of a foreign firm owning less than 50% of a national company compared with it owning 100% for the six aspects of national interests listed in Table 9. Two main conclusions are suggested by the pattern of responses.

TABLE 9
ATTITUDES ON JOINT VENTURES

	Average Scores of all Elites		
	Britain	France	Canada

Effects of foreign minority ownership as compared to 100% foreign ownership rated as worse (1) to better (7) for each factor.

Opportunities for X managers	5.0	4.5	5.6
X control of national affairs	4.9	4.4	5.3
X balance of payments	4.9	4.4	5.3
X national income	4.7	4.7	4.8
Opportunities for X investors	4.9	4.6	5.6
X industrial productivity	4.4	5.0	4.2
Average	4.6	4.6	5.1

Average of differences between lowest and highest ratings for the six host nation interests by each respondent.

Legislators	1.8	1.9	3.0
Government officials	1.6	1.9	2.6
Heads of firms	1.6	2.2	2.8
Labor leaders	1.9	1.9	2.5

First, although the attitudes are clearly favorable to joint ventures, they are not as strongly so as the prevalence of stated opinions and the character of some government policies would lead one to expect, especially in Britain and France.

The second point is the modest degree of differentiation shown in the European data at the bottom. In reality there are major differences in the effects. For example, joint ventures are often less productive because of technology communications problems (e.g. a score of 2 or 3), while host national investors almost always benefit (e.g. a score of 6). The survey shows that the Canadians make such significant distinctions, but the British and French tend to regard joint ventures as all-purpose devices that will help them fairly uniformly in many ways.

Over-all Attitudes Toward Foreign Firms

Among the four major subjects examined, the control and economic impacts stand out as being most important and having the most questionable results in the eyes of the elites. The loss of control over national affairs is clearly considered adverse, while the economic appraisals are mixed, generally favorable in overall terms but unfavorable when external payments are considered. The effects on workers are also considered quite important and, while the appraisals are varied, the general picture is favorable to the foreign firms. The opinions on cultural effects indicate that criticism of business influences leading to the "Americanization" of Canada and Europe are of doubtful significance. The elites rated this criterion distinctly lower than the others and were generally favorable in their judgments of the cultural impact of the firms.

Since the assessments on the two most important criteria (control and economics) tend toward the adverse side, it is notable that most respondents expressed an overall favorable opinion on the effects of the foreign firms. While there may be diverse, specific factors affecting this overall view, it seems quite likely that, for many respondents, it represents a "gut feel," a synthesis of assorted factual and emotional imputs into the mind. Thus, it would appear that there is among most of them an intuitive view that the foreign firms are beneficial which balances the somewhat negative views which one might compute by adding up their thoughts about the specific effects weighted by the importance attached to them.

The data also provide small but reinforcing evidences of the underlying nationalistic emotions which affect appraisals. In both the control and economic questions, it is clear that the judgments of the elites were not based entirely on tangible facts or basic logics. Thus the influence of nationalist reaction to external control and drain on national wealth which can be hypothesized from concepts of nationalism seems to be confirmed by the data.

Putting the evidences of intuitive overall appraisal and nationalist reaction together, we have an interesting combination of attitudes. It would appear that, among the developed nations, there is a generally receptive overall environment for foreign firms. However, always simmering beneath the surface are basic nationalist views, which are adverse to the firms and which are closely related to the two specific issues on which negative views are most evident—loss of control of national affairs and economic outflow. Recurring resistance to the firms based on this combination of specific issues and nationalist reaction is a natural expectation, therefore, despite the basically favorable overall appraisal.

REFERENCE

GENNARD, J. (1972) Multinational Corporations and British Labour. London: British North-American Committee.

The Military-Industrial Linkages of U.S.-Based Multinational Corporations

JONATHAN F. GALLOWAY
Department of Politics
Lake Forest College

Of the top 100 Department of Defense (DOD) contractors in fiscal year (FY) 1971, 39 were also multinational corporations, meaning that they held 25% or more of total equity interests in manufacturing enterprises located in six or more foreign countries at the end of 1963 (Vaupel and Curhan, 1969: 3)[1] More significantly, among the top 25 contractors, which accounted for 51% of prime contracts in 1971 and were by and large the same firms that were in the top 25 category in the late 1950s (Yarmolinsky, 1971: 251), 13 were multinational enterprises in the above sense. These 13 accounted for 25% of all prime contracts. The top 3 DOD contractors, which were multinationals also—General Dynamics, Lockheed, and General

1. This definition is useful in that the Harvard Business School has identified and done extensive research on 187 such firms. However, the definition is static and does not give a developmental, process-oriented view of the evolution of the multinational firm evolving through the following stages: (1) exporting to foreign countries, (2) establishing sales organizations abroad, (3) licensing patents to foreign firms, (4) establishing foreign manufacturing facilities, (5) multinationalizing management, and (6) multinationalizing ownership (Jacoby, 1970: 38).

AUTHOR'S NOTE: This article is a slightly revised version of a paper presented at the International Studies Association Annual Convention in Dallas, Texas, March 14-18, 1972. I wish to thank Robert Dixon, Samuel P. Huntington, Edward P. Levine, George Modelski, Steven Rosen, and Wesley B. Truitt for their comments and criticisms on this paper. I alone remain responsible for the analysis in the final version.

Electric—had over 13% of the contracts, amounting to over $4 billion in sales. Many data on the operations of the top defense contractors have recently become available, especially in light of studies by the Joint Economic Committee and the General Accounting Office (U.S. Congress, 1968-1969); but there is as yet no comparably comprehensive data on the international operations of American-based multinational firms. However, with the selective data that are now available, and especially if we are interested in reordering the priorities of American politics,[2] one can begin to make some interesting observations and speculative propositions concerning military-industrial linkages of American-based multinational corporations.

Before plunging into this labyrinth, one must briefly consider what is meant by the military-industrial complex, for the explicit linkage of the international operations of the nation's largest corporations with prime military contracts may evoke the image of a pervasive economic or military elite controlling American foreign policy. The concept of the military-industrial complex has been subjected to diverse definitions and interpretations. Scholars have argued about the validity of power elite, ruling class, pluralist, bureaucratic, and other models of military-industrial relationships. Rather than dismissing pluralist and elitist models and seeking one correct theory of the military-industrial complex as has been recently attempted (Lieberson, 1971; Slater and Nardin, 1971), this author prefers to view the military-industrial complex as an overarching concept like power, the state, or war. It is a general phenomenon which is composed of pluralist, elitist, and other elements *depending on the issue area.* All the seriously proposed views may be describing part of the beast we call the military-industrial complex, and they may be partially valid depending on the issue areas involved—foreign aid, arms sales, the strategic arms race, cost overruns, violence, genocidal wars, and so on. It

2. I believe it is the function of social scientists to make objective value judgments as well as describe, explain, and predict behavior. Thus I reject the following ethical theories: positivism and cultural relativism, an extreme form of which, individual relativism, seems very popular today. I also reject fundamentalist ethics and accept a type of contextual ethics.

is true that the subtheories of a general theory need to be tightened up, but they do not need to be discarded. However, such a general theory will not be attempted here, for our interest lies in examining economic and political data concerning only the multinational corporate aspects of the military-industrial complex.[3] Therefore, let us now return to the analysis of the convergence between DOD contractors and the American-based multinational enterprise, to be followed by an analysis of the consequences of the linkages that exist for certain issue areas.

Four Types of Defense Contractors

With the selective information that is now available, we can distinguish four types of defense contractors evaluated from the perspective of their sales abroad,[4] to the government, and to the domestic commercial market (see Table 1). There are those firms such as General Electric and ITT, which are significantly dependent on sales abroad and military sales. On the other hand, there are those firms like Lockheed and McDonnell-Douglas, which are more dependent on the government than GE and ITT but less dependent on international operations. Third, there are those firms which, although they are large defense contractors, depend very little on their sales to the government or abroad. AT&T, for instance, was the third largest contractor in FY 1971, having $1.2 billion in sales, but this amounted to only 5½% of Bell's total sales. Internationally, one may get an idea of AT&T's relative interests by pointing to the fact that the company has several hundred million in assets abroad but $54 billion at home. Fourth, there are those firms like Standard Oil of New Jersey, Ford, and Goodyear, which have significant sales abroad but whose sales to the government are less than 5%. From this breakdown into four types of DOD contractors, one

3. For a brief introduction to a general theory, see Galloway (1972). I am working on another version of this paper, focusing more on a general theory of the military-industrial complex.
4. Data on sales abroad by firms do not necessarily distinguish between export sales and sales by foreign subsidiaries. Export sales may be a stage on the way to establishing subsidiaries abroad, but this is not necessarily the case.

TABLE 1
MILITARY SALES AND FOREIGN SALES AS PERCENTAGE OF
TOTAL SALES OF SELECTED U.S. FIRMS

Fortune Rank, 1971	Firm	Percentage of total sales to:	
		Military[a]	Foreign[b]
1	General Motors	2	14[c]
2	Standard Oil (N.J.)	2	68
3	Ford Motor	3	36
4	General Electric	19	18
5	IBM	7	30[d]
7	Chrysler	4	21[c, d]
9	ITT	19	47
10	AT&T (Western Elec.)	9	n.a.
12	Standard Oil (Calif.)	n.a.	35[f]
18	RCA	16	6[g]
19	Goodyear Tire & Rubber	0[e]	30[d]
31	Lockheed	88	n.a.
39	North American-Rockwell	57	n.a.
45	McDonnell-Douglas	75	n.a.
75	TRW	11[e]	22[e]
128	General Tire	37	n.a.

a. 1960-1967 Department of Defense, as quoted in Melman (1970: 77-78).
b. 1967 as found in Rose (1968: 100).
c. Excludes Canada.
d. Includes export sales from the United States.
e. Data compiled from Department of Defense 100 companies list for FY 1970 and 1970 company reports.
f. Excludes western hemisphere.
g. 1965 as found in Weisskopf (1972: 433).
n.a. = not available. In all cases author estimates less than 5%.

can see that there is no one-to-one relationship between dependence on the governmental market and the international market.

In line with this observation, Murray Weidenbaum (1969: ch. 2), reminds us that we must avoid thinking of the top military contractors as a group possessing similar characteristics and behavior. The giants of American industry do not dominate the governmental market. Rather, it is the medium-sized firms which receive the largest share of orders. Thus, it is not General Motors, Ford, or Standard Oil of New Jersey, which are the core of the military-industrial complex, but Boeing, Lockheed, Hughes Aircraft, North American Rockwell, and the like, for the former have assets over $1 billion each, but receive 25% of the DOD contracts, while the latter have assets of $250-$999 million and receive 50% of the contracts.

It can be argued that this aggregate comparison ignores the question of what percentage of sales and profits are due to defense contracts. While Lockheed may be 90% dependent on government sales, if GE, ITT, RCA et al. are approximately 15-20% dependent on sales to the government, presumably they could not lightly afford to lose approximately one-fifth of their business. Also, it may be that these firms are even more dependent on governmental policy, for if they are significantly dependent on three markets—governmental, foreign, and domestic civilian—it stands to reason that their managements will be interested in preserving the dynamic equilibrium between these markets. If the equilibrium between these markets is upset, then the consequences for the firm may become unacceptable.

Another tendency which points to a close interconnection between firms and both the governmental and international markets concerns the dynamics of certain sectors of the economy rather than the size of firms or their relative assets and profits in different markets. That is, particular industries may be more dependent and become increasingly more tied to international financing and centralization of capital. It has been widely postulated that the advanced sectors of the economies of the world—i.e., computers, electronics in general, and chemicals—are becoming more multinational in character. If multinational corporations dominate in growth sectors concerned with increasingly sophisticated technologies, then, in the era of the qualitative arms race, it will be the multinational firms and the multinational consortia of government and business that will supply the defense needs of states. It may be postulated further that, to the extent that multinational corporations, which are either under the influence of foreign nations or are not under the control of nations at all, are supplying some of the defense needs of a state, then military defense in that state is being multinationalized. In fact, while it is often said that multinationalization of production is least apt to occur in military areas because no country wishes to be dependent on foreign interests for its defense, it is actually the case that cooperative projects in Europe have occurred more in the military than the civilian sphere (Behrman, 1971). Furthermore, the European defense market is partially controlled by American companies, and if one examines the licensing stage of the movement toward multinationalization rather than the ownership stage, one also sees a high degree of linkage (Harlow, 1967).

Multinational and Defense Industry Linkages

This indicates that close military-industrial relationships are not only an American phenomenon but a European phenomenon, too. But looking at the American situation more closely, we discover, by relating the top defense industries to the top multinational enterprises, that the following industries are found in both categories: transportation (including aerospace and automobiles), rubber, oil, electronics, and chemicals (see Table 2).

Aerospace is America's largest manufacturing industry, but it is the least multinational of the industries that are both multinational and defense-oriented. Only 4 of the 187 multinational enterprises in the Harvard study are aerospace firms whereas, in any given year, approximately 20 of the top DOD contractors are in the aircraft industry and about 15 in the missile business. However, as Horst (1972: 8) demonstrates, the largest firms in any industry are apt to be multinational, and the top aerospace DOD contractors are all in the *Fortune* list, most being ranked in the first 100. Nevertheless, there are several reasons why aerospace firms do not have many production facilities abroad: the cost of transporting finished products is low; very few foreign governments produce their own aircraft, so there are usually no tax or quota obstacles; and the American government's subsidies in R & D and capital expenditures make the United States a splendid place to do business. However, recently the rise of competition in the world aerospace market and the decline in sales to the domestic military market have affected the weight of these factors. The industry is becoming increasingly dependent on exports; these rose from $1,726 million in 1960 to $3,400 million in 1970 and accounted for approximately 14% of total sales of $24.8 billion (Aerospace

TABLE 2

A RANK ORDER COMPARISON OF DEFENSE LINKED AND
MULTINATIONAL INDUSTRIES

DOD[a] (SIC No.[b])	Total Con- tracts[c] $b	Multi- national[d] (SIC No.[b])	Sales Abroad[e] $b
Transportation equipment[f] (37 and 1925)	16.2	petroleum refining (29)	20.0
electrical machinery (36)	7.3	transportation equipment (37)	14.5
ordnance, except guided missiles (19)	4.7	chemicals and allied products (28)	10.2
nonelectrical machinery (35)	1.3	nonelectrical machinery (35)	8.2
instruments and related products (38)	1.1	food products (20)	5.4
primary and fabricated metals (33 and 34)	.9	electrical machinery (36)	5.3
petroleum refining (2911)	.6	primary and fabricated metals (33 and 34)	4.7
chemicals and allied products (28)	.4	paper and allied products (26)	2.5
fabricated rubber products (3069)	.2	rubber products (30)	2.1

a. 1968 data on shipments to DOD (U.S. Department of Commerce, 1970: 8-10).
b. SIC No. is Standard Industrial Classification number used by Department of Commerce.
c. Prime contracts and subcontracts for 1968 in rounded billions of dollars. Total of this sample is $32.6 billion as compared to $33.4 billion for all U.S. industries.
d. 1968 data on sales of foreign manufacturing facilities of industries included in this study compared with manufacturing sales of all U.S. foreign direct investors (U.S. Department of Commerce, 1972a: II,3).
e. 1968 sales of foreign subsidiaries in billions of dollars. Total of this sample is $72.9 billion as compared to $79.7 billion for all U.S. foreign direct investors.
f. This category includes the following industries: aircraft ($7.1 billion), aircraft engines and parts ($2.9 billion), aircraft propellers and parts ($2.2 billion), ship building and repairing ($1 billion), trucks (over $100 million), and complete guided missiles ($2.9 billion). NOTE: SIC No. 1925 is complete guided missiles which is not included in multinational category.

Industries Association of America, 1971: 2). In addition, as Harlow (1967) indicates, several top aerospace firms directly own considerable portions of certain important European defense industries. Aerospace is thus considerably more multinational than it was in 1963, the year on which the Harvard study bases its definition. However, there is no inevitability in this movement. The industry favors increased support from and participation by the government so that it will not have to form consortia with foreign interests, but, if this is not forthcoming, greater denationalization of the aerospace industry will probably occur (Harr, 1972: 270). In any case, while the almost total dependence of the aerospace industry on governmental sales is perfectly apparent, it may be said that dependence on foreign sales has been increasing and that preconditions exist for further movement toward multinationalization of production.

Another industry which ranks quite high on the Department of Defense prime contractor list, the Harvard Multinational Enterprise list, and the *Fortune* 500 list of 1971 is the automobile industry. This industry holds the first place on the multinational list, and third place on the defense list (see Table 3), and the companies in this industry also stand at the top of the *Fortune* list.

For the industry as a whole in 1969, total sales amounted to $92 billion. But the top firms were more dependent on the international market and productive system than was the industry at large. In 1970, 19% of General Motors' net earnings came from abroad, while 32.4% of its manufacturing was abroad. (The normal earnings abroad are approximately 8%, but strikes caused a dramatic upsurge in 1970. This fact may show the reliance of this company on the international market as a safety valve.) In the same year, Ford derived 24% of its total income from outside the United States and Canada, while 30.6% of its manufacturing was abroad. Of the 4 largest automobile firms, 3 were in the top 25 list of Department of Defense contractors—GM was 17; American Motors, 20; and Ford, 24 for fiscal year 1971, while Chrysler was 33. From this information and Table 1, we can see that, while the Big Four automobile corporations are in the DOD top 100 list and thus tied into the governmental market to some degree, they are more dependent on the international market. (However, this does not tell us about profits in the two markets, as profit figures are amalgamated and are often questionable.)

Closely tied to the successes and failures of the automobile industry is the rubber industry. Of the largest four rubber companies—B. F. Goodrich, Firestone, Goodyear, and Uniroyal—two are on the DOD top 100 list—Goodyear, 52; Uniroyal, 66.[5] Uniroyal is also dependent on the international market, for in 1970, 75% of its earnings came from foreign operations. Goodyear is expanding its foreign operations, which account for about 30% of its sales and income. An estimated 25% of the consolidated sales of Firestone is derived from abroad. B. F. Goodrich, the smallest of the big four, is also expanding its operations abroad (Standard & Poor's Industry Surveys, 1971: R185-R186).

In the case of the oil companies, we find that 4 of the largest 5 are on the DOD top 100 list, but all 4 number below the first 25. Standard Oil of New Jersey ranks 27, Standard Oil of California is 38, Mobil is 55, and Texaco is 44, while Gulf is not listed at all and sells only about 1% of its total products to the government. Thus, as with the automobile and rubber industries, we may conclude that the oil industry is more dependent on the international than on the governmental market.

The electronics industry, on the other hand, is more equally dependent on the governmental and international markets. Almost half of all electronic business during the last 7 years has been with the government. In 1970, the industry made total shipments of $24,290 million, and $11,687 million went to the government. The principal electronics companies—GE, ITT, Litton, RCA, Sperry Rand, Texas Instruments, and Westinghouse Electric—are all large defense contractors, all but Texas Instruments being in the top 25. Several of these companies do substantial business abroad, too, and are expanding their

5. General Tire & Rubber, the smallest of the rubber companies, is the largest DOD contractor (32) due to the contracts of its subsidiary, Aerojet General Corp.

operations. For instance, GE does about 19% of its business with the government and 18% abroad.

The chemical industry is similar to oil, rubber, and automobiles in being slightly defense-linked but significantly multinational. In 1970, total sales reached $45.1 billion. Of this amount, only $1.1 billion was sold to the federal government, over one-half went to the AEC and $274.1 million to the DOD. On the other hand, exports were three times as much as sales to the government, amounting to $3,826 million, and sales of foreign subsidiaries were even greater, amounting to $10.2 billion in 1968. Looking at the top 11 chemical firms in terms of 1970 sales, however, we find that 5 of them were also prime defense contractors for FY 1971, these being Olin, 30; FMC, 37; Hercules, 40; Thiokol (W. R. Grace), 43; Du Pont, 46. Furthermore, each of these 5 is a multinational enterprise according to the Harvard definition. Therefore, while the linkage of the whole chemical industry to the DOD is slight, some top firms in the industry are somewhat dependent on defense contracts. But these 5 firms are not in the top 25 on the DOD list as is the case with 3 of the top 4 auto companies.

Having briefly surveyed each of these important industries, let us now summarize the relations between the governmental/military, foreign, and domestic markets. For this purpose, Table 3 indicates the relative dependence of each industry on sales in the 3 markets. We see that the electronics industry fits into the first category of those developed from the data in Table 1–i.e., the industry is significantly dependent on foreign and military sales, bearing in mind that the top firms, in terms of the *Fortune* list, are most apt to be in each category. The aerospace industry appears to be moving from the second classification of large governmental, small foreign dependence, to the first. The automobile industry is a top defense industry from the point of view of the DOD list but not from its own sales perspective, while at the same time being considerably dependent on foreign markets for sales. Lastly, the oil refining, rubber, and chemical industries are in the fourth category of small governmental, large international dependence. Hence, from the point of view of military-industrial linkages, the electronics, aerospace, and, to a degree, the automobile industries are of especial interest.

Issue Areas and Multinational-Military Linkages

Let us now briefly examine several policy areas to see how firms and industries which have high stakes in both the governmental market and the international economy may influence and benefit from national policy decisions. George

TABLE 3

A COMPARISON OF GOVERNMENT (DOD) SALES, FOREIGN SALES
AND DOMESTIC SALES IN SIX INDUSTRIES (billions of dollars)

Industry	Government (DOD)			Foreign[a]		Domestic[b]		Total	
	$		%	$	%	$	%	$	%
Aerospace[c]	17.5	(14.6)	71	3.4	14	3.9	15	24.8	100
Electronic[d]	11.5[e]	(11.1)	46	3.6	15	9.7	39	24.8	100
Automobile[f]	1.3[e]	(1.1)	1	18.6	20	72.1	79	92.0	100
Oil[g]	.9[e]	(.8)	2	20.0	43	25.5	55	46.4	100
Rubber[h]	.4[e]	(.3)	4	2.5	26	6.7	70	9.5	100
Chemicals[i]	1.1	(.3)	2	14.0	31	30.0	67	45.1	100

a. The data in this column do not necessarily distinguish between foreign subsidiaries sales and export sales. Thus, there are no exact data for industries at large on their stages of multinationalization.

b. Arrived at by subtracting foreign sales and government sales from total sales.

c. 1970 data from Aerospace Industries Association of America, Inc. (1971-1972).

d. 1970 data from Standard & Poor's (1971: May 20, E11-E29).

e. Exact figures are available for DOD sales, FY 1971 (with the exception of oil, FY 1967). It is assumed that military sales account for 85% of all government sales.

f. 1969 data from Automobile Manufacturers Association, Inc. (1971). DOD sales calculated on the basis of the top four auto companies. Foreign calculated on the basis that export sales were 4.1 billion and subsidiary sales 14.5 billion in 1968.

g. 1966-1968 data. Sales to DOD are the FY 1967 combined sales of seven oil companies on DOD list. Foreign sales are the 1968 sales of foreign manufacturing facilities as estimated by U.S. Department of Commerce (1972: II, 3). Total sales are for 1966 (Vernon, 1971b: 14).

h. 1970 data from Standard & Poor's (1971: August 12, R191) for six rubber companies. The foreign sales are estimated on the basis that foreign sales of affiliates of Firestone, Goodyear, and Uniroyal have been 25, 30, and 75%, respectively.

i. 1970 data on total sales and exports from Standard & Poor's (1971: August 19, C23). 1970 data on government sales from U.S. Department of Commerce (1972b: 8-9). 1968 data on sales of foreign subsidiaries from U.S. Department of Commerce (1972a: II,3). Of foreign sales, $3.8 billion were exports; $10.2 billion those of foreign subsidiaries.

Modelski (1971) has argued that the evidence at hand "does not support the case for the existence of strong links between multinational business and war and military activities." To support this proposition, he demonstrates that in the 65 major armed conflicts for the period 1945-1970 there were relatively few instances of direct participation by multinational business. The evidence also confirms the conventional wisdom that multinational business avoids areas of political instability, for the number of subsidiaries of worldwide firms is much greater in areas of low conflict. The data at hand, however, may force us to conclusions which are not entirely warranted. Since World War II, there have been at least four cases of nonmajor armed conflicts associated with the activities of multinational firms— the CIA-sponsored coups in Iran in 1953, in Guatemala in 1954 and 1963, and in Bolivia in 1971, in addition to the seven major instances which Modelski mentions: Indonesia, Malaya, Algeria, Katanga, the Suez crisis, the Nigerian civil war, and the policies of the United States toward Castro's Cuba. In addition, the interests of multinational firms have been involved in trouble areas where the threat of force has affected the policies of foreign governments—e.g., the ITT/CIA/Chile case (Johnson et al., 1972). But, by its very nature, the role of subversion in the overthrow or maintenance of governments unfriendly or friendly to the interests of "private enterprise" cannot be thoroughly documented. Unless there are more Ellsbergs, Andersons, and Rosses and Wises, we shall only see some trees and not the forest, assuming that there is a forest.

The issue of whether overt military force or the threat of force has been brought to bear on foreign governments in the direct interests of multinational corporations is only part of the problem, however. In what economic areas—for example, tax policy, anti-trust legislation, compensation for nationalization, and the like—have the interests of multinational firms been advanced even if we lack complete data on the policy process during which particular decisions were made? Further, how have multinational enterprises influenced international organizations like the World Bank, the International Monetary Fund, and the Organization for Economic Cooperation and Development? One might hazard the proposition that while multinational firms favor corporatism at home—"socialism for the rich, free enterprise for the poor" (Mitchell, 1971)—they often favor free enterprise abroad because of the way that market is structured in their favor: in it, they are more equal than their competitors.

While it is true that, in terms of the numbers of subsidiaries and the value of investments, the attention of multinational firms has shifted from the poorer countries to the developed world, this does not mean that worldwide firms are not just as dependent on less-developed countries as previously, perhaps more so. One has to analyze the situation qualitatively as well as quantitatively. What matters for determining interdependence is not the ratio of direct investment abroad to direct investment at home, GNP/trade ratios, and so on, but as Richard Cooper (1972: 179) points out, "the *sensitivity* of economic transactions between two or more nations to economic developments within these nations." Thus, if the investments in Europe of American firms depend on the supply of raw materials or agricultural products from less-developed countries, then even if the stakes in Europe are greater, the stakes in the poorer countries are crucial. For instance, approximately 25% of American direct private investments in Europe are in oil. These operations depend on oil imports from the developing world. Consequently, it is not very enlightening to separate the two areas of investment if there are such essential linkages between them.

Military Aid and Sales

Let us now briefly consider the interconnections among foreign aid, defense business, and multinational enterprise. The aid program provides about $1 billion in sales annually for U.S. manufacturers and gives shipping companies about one-fourth of their total revenue from exports. In 1971, the Defense Department planned to award the following contracts as part of foreign military assistance: $175 million to McDonnell-Douglas for aircraft, $116 million to GE for aircraft engines, $61 million to Lockheed for aircraft and maintenance services, $89 million to Bell Helicopter for helicopters, $10 million to Chrysler for vehicles, and so on (Wall Street Journal, 1971). Furthermore, the Joint Economic Committee found that while the military assistance program allotted for FY 1970 totaled $409 *million,* the true total of military assistance in that year amounted to at least $2.9 *billion.* And Senator William Fulbright has introduced a table showing more than $6.9 billion in military sales and assistance for FY 1971, while the estimated total since 1945 comes to about $175 billion (U.S. Congress, 1971: 4-5, 50). What explains this huge program which is increasing and should increase more given the presuppositions of the Nixon Doctrine?

Conventional amoralistic theorizing on world politics has resulted in such spuriously hybrid normative-empirical propositions as "every country must (in the present international system) be accorded the right to define its national security needs as it thinks fit" (Gray, 1972: 155). This type of reasoning determines supposedly correct conclusions which consider arms sales and aid a necessary evil because of the competitive dynamics of the international system. But, while emphasizing political explanations—which explain everything in general and nothing in particular—these commentators see a certain part of this competition as economic involving beneficial multiplier effects upon the national economy, contributions to the balance of payments, dependence upon foreign sales for economic-scale production runs, and increased employment and profits (Gray, 1972: 168; Stanley and Pearton, 1971: 7, 71-72). Also, the administration reasons that, if the United States does not sell arms, other countries will. But a Senate Foreign Relations Committee staff study posits another explanation:

> If the United States were to lose its entire arms market in the underdeveloped world the impact on our overall balance-of-payments accounts would be small. Therefore, our justification for such sales must be based on the other considerations, such as influencing the development of local military elites or helping a country resist the threat of external aggressions [quoted in Melman, 1970: 94].

If one relates this justification for the arms sales policy to the stated objectives of the aid program in assisting the establishment of private enterprise economies in the underdeveloped countries, one can reasonably conclude that there is a self-reinforcing relationship between military contractors and American-based multinational corporations. The relationship is even closer, of course, if the two roles converge in the same company. Furthermore, 20 of the top 25 DOD contractors for FY 1971 were also on the list of major U.S. suppliers of weapons and equipment for the military assistance grant aid and sales program, and 11 of these 20 were on the Harvard multinational enterprise list (U.S. Congress, 1971: 57). Taking the total population of arms manufacturers, it has been found that the DOD has encouraged 1,480 out of some 1,500 total to sell abroad (Stanley and Pearton, 1971: 89).[6]

Conclusions

Having briefly examined a few of the issue areas that have been influenced by a convergence of the multinational enterprise with the military-industrial establishment (and there are others such as the arms race, and European defense organization), let us conclude by focusing and summarizing the arguments and then considering the options available for restructuring U.S. national priorities. It has been postulated that certain—but not all—major industries and the large corporations in these industries are dependent on the equilibrium between the defense market, foreign markets and the civilian market at home. To the extent that one market declines or is saturated, these firms and industries have an interest in expanding into the other markets. Furthermore, oligopolistic industries have a vested interest in seeing all markets grow. Currently, companies in the advanced defense sector of the economy are seemingly pressed to the wall by three factors: severe dependence on

6. While, after World War II, 70% of arms sales abroad were handled by the government rather than privately, this distinction breaks down if there is interpenetration of personnel and attitudes in the two sectors (Stanley and Pearton, 1971: 85, 92).

unpredictable technological innovations, extensive working capital requirements, and the leveling off of orders in the domestic defense market. (This last factor has become less important, given the FY 1973 DOD appropriations increase.) Military-oriented firms are thus impelled to seek out other markets; some of these will be abroad. These firms will have to search for more sources of capital; some of these will be abroad.

Under what conditions might ties between multinational corporations and industries and military-oriented firms and industries become weaker, in both the United States and the North Atlantic area? In answer to this complex question, let me be more general than precise. Nationalism may counter the tendencies toward the internationalization of capital, pro- duction, and research and development, especially insofar as the defense functions of sovereign states are concerned. On the other hand, in the era of the qualitative arms race, huge capital requirements for advancements in weapons technology may compel states to forego ideas of military self-sufficiency. Furthermore, the internationalization of production in certain civilian areas—e.g., commercial airplanes, computers, nuclear energy, will inevitably have military side effects. Thus, these two considerations may cause one to foresee a partial multi- nationalization of the defense infrastructures of certain coun- tries, especially those in the North Atlantic area. The market for the output of this new productive center will not be, as argued above, restricted to this one area; many less-developed states will continue their conventional arms races with the leftover inventories of the great powers.

Through which conscious policies might the United States control for the increasing interdependence of the multinational enterprise and the military-industrial establishment (given the fact that a solution to the problem of the military-industrial complex may involve attacking it on all fronts and in all issue areas)? Liberals might posit at least five ways to control the disadvantageous consequences of this new convergence. In the first place, there might be increased public control over the corporation through requiring federal incorporation, as suggested by Ralph Nader (1971). Second, one might nationalize the defense industries as suggested by John Kenneth Galbraith (1969). Third, a renewed emphasis on conversion might be undertaken. Fourth, one might suggest that there be an international code for multinational enterprise and perhaps an international charter for firms (Reisman, 1971; Ball, 1968). And last, liberals and conservatives might put their hopes on further sessions of SALT as well as conventional arms limitations negotiations. What is the likelihood that any or all of these policies will be adopted? It does not seem that corporations will be required to receive federal charters. What chance is there that Congress will change incorporation laws against the intensive efforts of corporate lobbyists? Second, nationalization of defense industries smacks too much of socialism and communism to be politically feasible. Third, conversion has by and large failed in the past. It does not meet the requirements and habits of those businesses dependent on the defense market. The fourth suggestion—an international code for business—is too legalistic an approach to regulation. As with the Corrupt Practices Act domestically, it may be predicted that there will be many loopholes and but little enforcement. The last approach seems to present the greatest hope for controlling arms sales and races, given the success of SALT I. On the other hand, while these talks have slowed down one part of the strategic arms race, they have not ended it, and, ironically, the gambit of negotiating from strength means that arms control negotiations are being used to fuel the arms race.

It thus appears that liberal solutions for the control of the military-industrial linkages of the multinational corporation will not be adopted, or, if they are, they will not have any systematic impact on the direction of American policies. The domestic corporation is often superior to the power of states in the American federal system, and, in a world of states, the multinational corporation may act likewise, pursuing its equivalent policies of divide and rule, balance of power, and containment and expansion toward at least the majority of the states of the world. The nation-state, especially the great and superpowers, will not be replaced, but the dynamics of the oligopolistic, technological, and profit imperatives could very well make multinational enterprises their coterminous and contiguous partners. It is thus incorrect to stress a conflict between states and corporations or economics and politics for what we are viewing is a penetrated system of symbiotic relationships where the important boundaries are increasingly functional and associational rather than territorial. Liberal politics may only be able to tinker with the machinery of this emerging world order, unless a series of incremental changes can eventually create a systematic transformation of the priorities toward more socially useful programs in transportation, housing, health, development in the Third World, and the like.

What can be said of the radical solutions to the disorders and discontents of our times? Radical solutions may work, but we shall never know, for it is even less likely that there will be revolution in the United States than that there will be a federal chartering of corporations. Thus, we and the world may be stuck with a system of priorities which results in arms races, arms sales, energy crises, pollution, and so on for the rest of the century. Political scientists should criticize these developments as deranged and not succumb to individual relativism on moral questions or to the amoralistic theorizing which characterizes much of the discipline. To the extent that this normative position and its empirical supports are valid, then scholars could have some small, hopefully cumulative impact on the future priorities of American politics.

REFERENCES

Aerospace Industries Association of America, Inc. (1971) Aerospace Facts and Figures 1971/72. New York.

Automobile Manufacturers Association, Inc. (1971) 1979 Automobile Facts and Figures. Washington, D.C.

BALL, G. W. (1968) "Making world corporations into world citizens." War-Peace Report (October).

BEHRMAN, J. N. (1971) "Multinational production consortia: lessons from NATO experience." U.S. Department of State Publication 8593, August.

COOPER, R. (1972) "Economic interdependence and foreign policy in the seventies." World Politics 24, 2: 159-181.

Fortune (1972) "The Fortune directory of the 500 largest industrial corporations." (May): 188.

GALBRAITH, J. K. (1969) "The big defense firms are really public firms." New York Times Magazine (November 16): 50, 162-176.

GALLOWAY, J. F. (1972) "Multinational corporations and the military-industrial complex." Presented at the International Studies Association Annual Convention, Dallas, March.

GRAY, C. S. (1972) "Traffic control for the arms trade." Foreign Policy 6 (Spring): 153-169.

HARLOW, C.J.E. (1967) "The European armaments base: a survey." London Institute for Strategic Studies, June, July.

HARR, K. G., Jr. (1972) "Technology and trade." Vital Speeches (February 15): 267-270.

HORST, T. (1972) "Firm and industry determinants of the decision to invest abroad: an empirical study." Harvard Institute of Economic Research Discussion Paper 231, March.

JACOBY, N. H. (1970) "The multinational corporation." Center Magazine 3 (May): 37-55.

JOHNSON, D. L., J. POLLOCK, and J. SWEENEY (1972) "ITT and the CIA: the making of a foreign policy." Progressive (May): 15-17.

LIEBERSON, S. (1971) "An empirical study of military-industrial linkages." Amer. J. of Sociology 76 (January): 562-584.

MELMAN, S. (1970) Pentagon Capitalism. New York: McGraw-Hill.

MITCHELL, W. C. (1971) Public Choice in America. Chicago: Markham.

MODELSKI, G. (1971) "Multinational business: a global perspective." Presented at the One Hundred Thirty-Ninth Meeting of the American Association for the Advancement of Science, Philadelphia

NADER, R. (1971) New York Times (January 24): Section 3, 1, 9.

OSTERBERG, D. and F. AJAMI (1971) "The multinational corporation: expanding the frontiers of world politics." J. of Conflict Resolution 15 (December): 457-470.

REISMAN, M. (1971) "Polaroid power." Foreign Policy 4: 101-110.

ROSE, S. (1968) "The rewarding strategies of multinationalism." Fortune (September 15).

SLATER, J. and T. NARDIN (1971) "The concept of a military-industrial complex." Presented at the Sixty-Seventh Annual Meeting of the American Political Science Association, Chicago, September.

Standard & Poor's (1971) Industry Surveys.

STANLEY, J. and M. PEARTON (1971) The International Trade in Arms. New York: Praeger.

U.S. Department of Commerce (1972a) The Multinational Corporation. Washington, D.C.: Government Printing Office.

––– (1972b) "Shipments of defense-oriented industries, 1970." Series MA-175(70)-1, June.

––– (1970) "Shipments of defense-oriented industries, 1968." Series MA-175(68)-2, November 20.

U.S. Congress (1968 and 1969) "Hearings and report, economics of military procurement." Joint Economic Committee, Subcommittee on Economy in Government. Ninetieth Congress, Second Session; Ninety-First Congress, First Session.

——— (1971) "Hearings, economic issues in military assistance." Joint Economic Committee, Subcommittee on Economy in Government. Ninety-Second Congress, First Session.

VAUPEL, J. W. and J. P. CURHAN (1969) The Making of Multinational Enterprise. Boston: Harvard Graduate School of Business Administration.

VERNON, R. (1971) Sovereignty at Bay. New York: Basic Books.

Wall Street Journal (1971) November 3.

WEIDENBAUM, M. (1969) The Modern Public Sector. New York: Basic Books.

——— (1963) "The transferability of defense industry resources to civilian use," pp. 101-113 in R. E. Bolton (ed.) Defense and Disarmament. Englewood Cliffs, N.J.: Prentice-Hall.

WEISSKOPF, T. E. (1972) "United States foreign private investment: an empirical survey," pp. 426-435 in R. C. Edwards et al. (eds.) The Capitalist System: A Radical Analysis of American Society. Englewood Cliffs, N.J.: Prentice-Hall.

YARMOLINSKY, A. (1971) The Military Establishment. New York: Harper & Row.

Corporate Giants

Some Global Social Costs

FOUAD AJAMI

Department of Political Science
University of Washington

Concentration and the Global Marketplace

Some projections into the future of the world economy depict an increasing rate of economic concentration, inviting serious thoughts as to its ability to provide for human welfare and to maintain a reasonable degree of diversity and pluralism in the world social system. Howard Perlmutter (1969, 1968) advances what he calls the "300-Hypothesis," a prediction that the global system of the future will be dominated by 300 or so giant enterprises. Economist Stephen Hymer (1970) propounds the same hypothesis and argues that present trends could produce a regime of 300 or 400 multinational corporations controlling 60 to 70% of the world industrial output. And Richard Barber's (1970) recent discussion of concentration in the American economy contends that "the entire industrialized world will soon be characterized by as high a degree of concentration as now prevails in the United States." By 1980, concludes Barber (1970: 264), "three hundred corporations will control 75 percent of the world's manufacturing assets."[1]

1. One can quarrel with these estimates and with the logic upon which they are based. They are linear projections premised upon current growth rates, and, as such,

AUTHOR'S NOTE: For invaluable assistance and encouragement I am grateful to Steven DeLue, Vicki Ajami, David Osterberg, and William Thompson.

Indeed, the complete resignation with which industrial concentration has come to be viewed conveys a sense of doom and helplessness in the face of irreversible forces that are beyond the limits of human will and human control. Galbraith's (1967) analysis, for example, leaves us little choice or maneuverability; industrial concentration and monopoly are portrayed as the natural state of affairs intrinsic to an industrial "maturation" process where the giant corporation is the mature form of industrial enterprise. Robert Rowthorn's (with Hymer, 1971: 3, 102) competent study is equally deterministic, and here the increase in the level of economic concentration is taken for granted as something that "increases indefinitely over time." Perhaps more revealing is the way in which those who profess a certain antipathy toward the concentration of economic power seem to be constrained in their imagination and wedded to the giant enterprise as the dominant mode of industrial organization in today's and future world orders. It is within this intellectual orientation that Raymond Vernon (1971: 273) expresses his own aversion to the concentration of economic power and in the same breath maintains that "the possibility that societies may be organized in small units with limited power seems implausible."

Such arguments are a counsel of despair, for economic concentration and oligopoly are neither inevitable nor necessarily intrinsic to an efficient industrial order. They are organizational strategies and weapons in the quest for power and control on the part of corporate giants bent upon eliminating competition, securing higher rates of return, and wielding greater power and influence over their environment. To paraphrase Modelski (1971: 6), they are "responses to the way in which the world is (or is not) organized." Industrial giants here behave much in the same manner that great powers do in the world political system, carving out spheres of influence, asserting their will upon as wide a range of issues as

their predictive capacity can be called into question. However, worldwide concentration due to mergers, internal growth, and direct foreign investment is a principal feature of the current world industrial order.

possible and securing the loyalty and compliance of as much of the world's populace as their resources and capabilities will permit. Both try to make the world in their own image, and, in the process, short-range organizational goals prevail while world order and the world public interest are negatively affected. In their attempt to increase the range of organizational certainty and dominance, both forms of organization seriously undermine the prospects for the free and legitimate competition of alternative visions and products in the world political and economic marketplace.

The questions that oligopoly and concentration raise are, of course, old and familiar ones.[2] and they have been a source of contention and controversy dating back to early Marxist thought and formulations. But Marxist thought, in its total rejection of capitalism as a mode of production and social organization, never came to grips with the day-to-day impact and costs of concentration and oligopoly (e.g., Baran and Sweezy, 1966). Dismissing the entire system as "carrying the seeds of its own destruction," opportunities for reform were inevitably overlooked and so were a whole host of tangible though important outcomes associated with oligopoly that confront men and women in a market where they have very little freedom, choice, and power. Nor, for that matter, did Marxists persuasively demonstrate that state monopoly solves the problems associated with the unchecked power of the oligopolists in a private market. But the old questions need to be revived and globalized given the increasing power and dominance of multinational giants and the globalization of the market and its tranformation into what Peter Drucker (1969: 77-101) uncritically and enthusiastically labels the "Global Shopping Center." And if this shopping center is being increasingly controlled by a small number of corporate giants, and competition within it curtailed through diversification, mergers, acquisitions, and elimination of present and potential

2. Several excellent works on oligopoly helped clarify my thinking and influence my orientation: Shepherd's (1970) Study; the Nader Study Group Report on Antitrust Enforcement (Green, 1971); and Hymer (1970).

competitors, as the sparse available evidence currently indicates, then the coming age of the multinational giants is hardly a cause for relief and inspiration. The old questions thus acquire a sense of urgency, novelty, and, more importantly, a global dimension.

Data about oligopoly and concentration in world markets are notoriously scarce and difficult to come by, which, in itself, is a sad commentary on the state of the art. Markets are still considered coextensive with nations, and the absence of global data is only a manifestation of a much broader and more serious problem: the world public interest is inadequately provided for by the current structure and priorities of the international system. One thing that can be stated with a reasonable degree of certainty at this time, however, is that the process of direct foreign investment and the growing global nature of the market seem to have set in motion particular forces conducive to higher levels of seller concentration, and, in that sense, one would have to concur with Hymer's (1970: 443) assessment that "the world level of concentration is much higher than it would be if foreign investment and domestic mergers were restricted." Yet throughout the industrialized world, the fascination with size and growth seems to preclude the possibility of halting or reversing the process of industrial concentration, so easily detected by cursory examinations of comparative data.[3] At any rate, Bain's (1966) seminal work on comparative concentration should have long shattered the illusion that concentration is unique to any national economy, or that it is a problem that can be primarily solved through the acts and decisions of national authorities. Comparing the degree of concentration in the other seven to its level in the United States, Bain found market concentration slightly lower in the United Kingdom, slightly higher in Japan, moderately higher in France and Italy and much higher in Canada, India, and Sweden.

3. The level of concentration in advanced industrialized countries has been documented in reports by the U.S. Senate Subcommittee on Antitrust and Monopoly, the Fair Trade Commission in Japan, the Monopolies Commission in the U.K., the Task Force on the Structure of Canadian Industry, and other standard sources.

Multinationalism: A Domain for Giantism

If the national thrust is toward giantism, and if the national authorities in the most economically visible and important countries show no inclination toward either halting or reversing concentration, then their unwillingness to curb it at the global level is a given that can be easily detected and understood. As a matter of fact, national authorities are anxious advocates of corporate giantism in the world economy, even if they are hostile to it in the domestic arena. The logic here is quite perverted and reminds one of the logic and the spiral that fuel the arms race. National governments maintain that, though they do not favor economic concentration, the giantism of corporations registered elsewhere can only be met by allowing and even officially encouraging the formation of corporate giants that can meet international competition. Carried to its fullest implications, then, world consumers are denied the same protection—admittedly ineffective—extended to their domestic counterparts. The world marketplace, then, if juxtaposed to its domestic equivalent, is probably more harsh, less regulated, and pays much less attention to the welfare of its consumers. These conclusions invite pessimism and create serious doubts as to whether the globalization of the economy through the growth of giants and super-firms is indeed as worthy of enthusiasm and support as its advocates have contended.

In Europe, for example, ever since Servan-Schreiber popularized the notion of the American challenge, a consensus has been created around the virtues of bigness and giantism. There is undoubtedly a greater "need for larger size in European business," concluded a study by two European economists (Swann and McLachlan, 1967: 54), and Rainer Hellmann's (1970) argument is basically similar. Europe's future lies in its ability to emulate the American invader: mergers and giantism. If European firms are ever to make significant inroads into the American market—a survival requirement—they have to diversify and grow in size, Hellmann concluded. Size, the consensus goes, confers market power, provides capital for further growth, and eliminates uncertainty. Rarely, if ever, are the costs and dislocations associated with size mentioned or elaborated upon.

Multinationalism invites bigness in other ways, and one could safely argue that its vehicle—direct foreign investment—is essentially the domain of corporate giants. A survey completed in 1960 by the Department of Commerce revealed that 143 firms accounted for 81% of total U.S. overseas manufacturing investments. Raymond Vernon's (1971: 18) study completed a decade later confirmed this concentration: his sample of 187 American-based multinational giants controlled as much as 80% of the liquid overseas assets of American companies.[4] And the investment activities of firms located in other countries evidence an even higher degree of concentration. The Task Force on the Structure of Canadian Industry (1968: 349) revealed that "the 13 largest firms involved accounted for 70 percent of such investment abroad in 1963. The next 8 largest firms for 7 percent, the next 38 largest for 12 percent, and the remaining 300-350 firms for 11 percent." In other words, 59 companies account for the bulk of Canada's overseas investment, an overwhelming 89%. The "Big Ten" enterprises[5] in Japan that account for 62% of its imports and 47% of its exports were responsible for as much as 80% of Japanese investment contracts in foreign countries (Ozawa, 1971). British investments also confirm the dominance of the giants: in 1962, 46 firms accounted for an impressive 71% of all British overseas investments in manufacturing (Reddaway, 1967).

The type of industries that the multinational giants participate in are also conducive to oligopoly and concentration. Chemicals, engineering, automotive, and petroleum industries, to name a few, are capital-intensive industries which require heavy capital outlays, and, as such, are characterized by high entry barriers and conditions that facilitate their dominance by a handful of firms.

4. Citing the September 1969 issue of Fortune, Perlmutter (1969: 63) tells of a statement made by an official of the French government: "By the year 2000, there will be 200 firms. We want ten to be French."

5. The Big Ten enterprises are the following giant trading companies: Mitsubishi, Mitsui, Marubeni-Iida, C. Itoh, Nissho-Iwai, Toyo Menka, Sumitomo, Nichimen, Kanematsu-Gosho, and Ataka.

By now the logic of the argument being pursued here should have become clear and evident: the linkage between multinationalism (as advanced through direct foreign investment) and increasing worldwide concentration is causal and direct. Three causative factors are singled out:

(1) Governments are unwilling to put firms based within their boundaries at a size disadvantage and tend to view the world economy as a free-for-all game.
(2) Direct foreign investment is principally the activity of giants.
(3) The industries in which the giants participate are conducive to concentration.

The last partly reflects the self-fulfilling prophecies of the giant oligopolists. Markets are structured in a way that prevents entry, curtails competition, and curbs the growth of smaller firms.

The correlation between oligopoly and the participation of multinational giants which has been contended here was confirmed by an analysis of 19 2-digit industry groups in Canada for 1964 (Task Force on the Structure of Canadian Industry, 1968· 426-427). With few exceptions, foreign (mostly U.S.) control positively and significantly correlated with higher levels of concentration.

World consumers, should present trends continue, can look forward to higher levels of concentration and oligopoly in more centralized and less pluralistic markets, controlled respectively by a few multinational giants. The features and costs of such oligopoly deserve urgent concern, a search for remedies, but more fundamentally, they call for basic knowledge and information which are the prerequisites of enlightened policy.

Some Costs and Features of Global Oligopoly

CULTURAL DOMINANCE AND CENTRALIZATION

On a general level, oligopoly is quite detrimental to the potentialities for global pluralism and diversity. The value of pluralism obviously depends upon the premium one places on it, and so far the oligopolists seem to show little tolerance for diversity and tend to behave as all large-scale organizations do when confronted with a complex environment: they attempt to increase certainty by reducing complexity and by wielding power and dominance. While the costs of such a strategy will be shared and felt by most, the burden is heaviest on non-Western cultures, where societies are open to currents, products, and styles over which they have little or no control. Hymer (1970: 446) has aptly noted that the dominance of the giants will confine most of the world "to the status of provincial capitals, towns, and villages in the New Imperial System. Income, status, authority and consumption patterns will radiate out from the centers in a declining fashion and the hinterland will be denied independence and equality." The oligopolists, in this sense, through the power to reach the hinterland and to market their products (and the values and life styles that go with them), will "enfranchise" the world's underprivileged majority. But the new constituency will lose its autonomy and freedom, while its ability to share the benefits of its membership in the corporate system would remain far from certain.

Somewhat below the preceding level of generalization, there are multiple features associated with oligopoly which merit attention and concern, and which, in a way, could be more easily and directly attributed to it. Most of the arguments discussed here, it should be noted, should be placed in the context of a massive literature on oligopoly and market structure that is rich in controversy and passionately contested opinions. Oligopoly has been praised and condemned, and the critics have been as eloquent and forceful in the presentation of arguments and data as the defenders.[6] All explanations thus— including this one—are partly selective in the way they perceive the subject and interpret the evidence.

6. For an appreciation of the differing perspectives and arguments, see Shepherd (1970), Scherer (1970), McGee (1971), Green (1971), and an article by Adelman (1970) which ends up contending that economic concentration is not such serious a problem as to merit much attention and controversy, a position with which I find myself in total disagreement.

TECHNOLOGICAL AND PRODUCT INNOVATION

From Schumpeter (1942) to Galbraith (1967), economists have lavished praise upon the large firm, notably upon its ability to provide for economies of scale, technological efficiency, and rapid growth. In the business folklore, despite the lip service paid to the virtues of competition, bigness was always admired, and the prevailing ideology has traditionally maintained that bigness does not necessarily preclude competition (Sutton et al., 1962). More recent evidence ought to sober this optimism and cast serious doubt upon the ability of large firms to provide for growth and technological innovation. The controversy surrounding technological innovation lies at the heart of the matter. Refuting it—if that is ever possible—means undermining the raison d'être of mergers, acquisitions, and bigness.

As directly related to the multinationals, the technology argument has recently surfaced: large multinationals will transfer technology to the underdeveloped world and will thus aid in its growth, development, and integration into the modern world economy (Quinn, 1969). Large firms can afford greater R&D expenditures, the reasoning goes, and as such are more likely to be technologically innovative and productive. So much was confirmed by Vernon's (1971) data. His sample of 187 multinational firms dedicated 2.48% of their sales for R&D purposes; the remainder of *Fortune's* list spent 1.85%, and the average for all American manufacturing enterprises was a comparatively low 1.29% (Vernon, 1971: 8-9).

The Nader Study Group Report (Green, 1971) and other empirical evidence surveyed, principally generated by studies in the American context, seem to stand in complete antithesis to the technological innovation argument. Size may, in fact, detract from inventive output instead of enhancing it. Vested interest due to size and bureaucratic inertia may suppress instead of spur innovation. The record of the automotive industry in the antipollution field is an excellent example: the stakes are so overwhelming and the position of the industry is so entrenched that a major undertaking on the antipollution front—let alone the development of alternative transportation systems—has been systematically resisted and ruled out. Instead, annual models are offered, along with different gadgets and gimmicks to replace genuine product competition. On a different industry, the Nader group quotes a former vice president of General Electric, the late T. K. Guinn, as saying that he knew of no original product invention in household appliances that was developed by GE or any of the other giants. Their record, says Quinn (1971: 47), "is one of moving in, buying out, and absorbing the smaller concerns."

Rather than using absolute or relative R&D figures, Scherer (1965) used the number of patents as an index of inventive output. Taking a sample of 448 companies, selected from *Fortune's* 500, he found a negative correlation between size and innovative capability. His findings raise doubts as to whether the big, monopolistic, conglomerate corporation is an efficient agent of technological change. Using the same index, Watson and Holman (1967) found that the giant firms do not generally produce as many patented inventions per million dollars of government-funded research as the medium-sized and smaller firms. One finds the performance of the giants rather disappointing.

Besides questioning the intensity and productivity of corporate R&D expenditures, one can (on different normative grounds) question its priorities and commitments. Berg's (1972) analysis of the international food industry is quite alarming. Despite world hunger and malnutrition, the giants of the international food industry, (Swift, Unilever, General Foods, Coca-Cola, and so on) have so far failed to confront these urgent problems. Thousands of food products are annually introduced into the market: few are aimed at the poor or packaged and processed at costs they can afford. "For all the technical ingenuity that has gone into the development of new products, corporate technologists have not yet been able to come up with a food that can be sold commercially for a profit and still be priced low enough to reach and help the masses of people who need it most" (Berg, 1972: 134). In India, for example, a country where the mere feeding of people is probably the top national priority, food companies conceded that the products introduced were aimed at middle- and upper-income levels, where the money and the purchasing power are located. Thus, despite the global shortage of protein, the food companies' laboratories are busy in a race to make their products more appealing and glamorous, in order to capture an essentially affluent audience. The race between Hunt-Wesson Food's snack-pack single portion canned puddings and General Food's Jell-O brand puddings is an excellent illustration. One wonders how much longer scarce resources can be wasted when the majority of the world's population cannot be guaranteed mere subsistence.

Georg Borgstrom (1967) adequately, though unfortunately, contends that the world's prospects for mass starvation are remarkably high and is even more sharply critical of the international food companies and their unwillingness to meet the pressing challenge. The investment activities of the international food industry, concluded Borgstron (1967: 365-366), "show little sign of any concern for coping with the vexing intricacies of world feeding. There is, rather, evidence of an unmistakable empire-building by large-scale mergers on the international scene."

Furthermore, the technology transfer argument, even if accepted as an outcome of corporate giantism, is probably undesirable in the global industrial system. Technological innovation, as it radiates from few industrial centers, and from the laboratories of a small number of corporations and states, probably stunts and stifles innovation capabilities in the non-Western world. Easily available from the international giants, there is little incentive or room for innovation in what will increasingly become the recipient and respository of the inventive output of others. Social growth as such would be more increasingly denied to the Third World, and with it the possibilities for innovation and creativity.

To recapitulate, the hypothesis that giants are responsible for product and technological innovation is found wanting. It is rejected principally for three reasons. First, it does not stand the test of empirical evidence; probably the reverse argument could be more easily made. Second, the priorities and direction of the giants' innovation can be seriously questioned, for the thrust of their effort seems to be directed toward luxury and ornament. Finally, the centralization of innovation is detrimental to a more pluralist and diffuse structure of creativity and innovative output in the global system.

PROFITS AND PRICES

Oligopoly confers market power upon the giants, and that ultimately means more profit. The after-tax earnings of Vernon's (1971: 8) sample of 187 multinationals for 1964 were 13.3%; for the remainder of *Fortune's* 500, 11.1%; and for U.S. manufacturing enterprises not on *Fortune's* list of 500, only 9.1%.

Not only do corporate giants earn more on their investments—largely because of administered prices and targeted returns—but they are also less subject to the fluctuations and pressures of the market, particularly in relatively inelastic markets. In these, the consumer is least sovereign, and the oligopolists' power is excessive and overwhelming. The international petroleum industry, a classic and important illustration of international oligopoly, is a salient case in point. The structure of the industry and its dominance by the "seven majors" has for long operated against the interest and welfare of world consumers. As late as 1966, the "seven majors" accounted for 76% of gross crude oil production and 61% of the refinery throughput of the market outside North America and the Communist countries (Penrose, 1968: 78). The same seven also dominate the Canadian and American markets and control all the stages of the world oil industry from the production of crude oil to the marketing of refined products. Their policies, conducted in close consultation with one another, have a significant impact upon world consumers, in a relatively inelastic market, where oil fuels the industrial machinery, powers automobiles that have become virtually indispensable, and heats dwelling units. The power of the seven majors has long been felt by consumers throughout the world. A conservative estimate by the U.S. Cabinet Task Force on Oil Import Control (1970), put the cost of the oil import quota—a political favor extracted by the giants—to the American consumers somewhere in the range of $5-7 billion per year. Michael Tanzer's (1969) study of the political economy of oil demonstrates that the industry has rarely, if ever, taken the interests of underdeveloped consumers into consideration. India's oil imports are three-fourths as large as its food imports and drain its foreign exchange, yet the structure of international oil is not really responsive to its needs and aspirations. Oligopolistic profit margins and returns accrue to the giants largely at the expense of relatively weak and ineffective consumers. Table 1 compares the profits of the giants with the averages realized by other companies engaged in the same markets.

From a global perspective, these rates of return tend to have a negative impact upon the prospects for a more egalitarian and even distribution of world income. Their redistributive function is quite regressive, for corporate profit redistributes wealth from the less to the more affluent sectors of the world population within and across nations. The holding of corporate stock has remained, despite the slogan of peoples' capitalism, an elite activity, so to speak. Corporate profit then not only transfers wealth from poor to rich countries (because of the national origin of the firms involved) but to a very small segment of the population of the rich countries and a much smaller number of large institutional investors (e.g. pension and mutual funds, insurance companies, and, to a lesser extent, churches, universities, and private foundations). This is probably one of the most serious and disruptive costs of global oligopoly. Thus the multinational giants, instead of contributing to the economic development and growth of the Third World as their advocates have claimed, are probably enlarging the gap between the rich and the poor, and aggravating the inequities in the distribution of world wealth and resources.

TABLE 1

RATES OF PROFITS ON SHAREHOLDERS EQUITY 1961-1965 IN SELECTED MARKETS (in percentages)

Industry and Leading Firms	Rates of Profits	Other firms
Motor Vehicles		8.3
General Motors	21.7	
Ford Motors	13.8	
Chrysler	13.5	
Computers		7.2
IBM	19.5	
Petroleum Refining		9.3
Standard Oil of New Jersey	12.1	
Texaco	15.5	
Mobil	8.7	
Gulf	11.1	
Tires and Tubes		6.8
Goodyear	11.7	
Firestone	11.2	
U.S. Rubber	7.8	
Dairy Products		9.0
National Dairy	11.3	
Borden	10.9	
Carnation	11.8	

SOURCE: Adopted from Shepherd (1970: 192-195) and the Federal Trade Commission, (1967) RATES OF RETURN ON IDENTICAL FIRMS IN SELECTED MANUFACTURING INDUSTRIES, 1940, 1947-1965. Washington, D.C.: Federal Trade Commission.

PRODUCT DIFFERENTIATION AND
LARGE-SCALE ADVERTISING

Among its other virtues or costs—depending upon one's orientation—large size is also advertising power. This power includes the ability to mold and create consumer wants, to secure consumer loyalty and a faithful clientele, as well as the ability to foster and strengthen organizational identity in an age of complex organizations. Few governments can indeed hope for as great a control upon the communication media and upon the perceptual world of their citizenry as the giant corporations exercise in their domain. Under the guise of private enterprise, the world communication media have become avenues for corporate products and messages, and for the transmission of corporate information. "The international community" writes

Herbert Schiller (1971: 53) "is being inundated by a stream of commercial messages that derive from the marketing requirements of (mostly) American multinational companies. The structure of national communications systems and the programming they offer are being transformed according to the specifications of international marketeers."

In both France and Canada, in what might indeed be a curious phenomenon, the largest advertisers and contributors to the media have been the U.S.-based multinationals and the two governments in their respective boundaries. Both the giant multinationals and the nation-state are thus apparently busy molding the values of the world's populations by monopolizing a resource which ought to be more freely, broadly, and openly utilized.

Advertising is fundamental to the position of the oligopolist (Comanor and Wilson, 1969). It might be a more adequate incentive for bigness than the presumed economies of scale advantage. As the giants exhaust the economies of scale and are much bigger than the minimum scale required for efficient and relatively cheap unit production, advertising power is definitely behind bigness, both as a cause and a function of it. Advertising is monopoly on information and products, and it requires large expenditures because of the prohibitive costs of TV time, newspaper space, and the like. The large advertiser is more secure because his ability to persuade as well as to counter-advertise (against public interest groups, government charges, and so on) is much greater than that of small firms and, all too often, than that of governments and public interest groups.

A certain level of advertising is needed to help the consumer make certain choices: as such, it serves an information function. But the level of advertising that the giants engage in is not only wasteful but also quite deceptive in content. Unwilling to engage in genuine product and quality competition, clever ads become the order of the day, and the consumer eventually suffers. In attempting to differentiate otherwise similar products, Anacin was backed in 1970 with $27 million and Bufferin with $14 million, to cite just one example. The result is inflated prices and unjustifiable claims.

And as Schiller (1971) has noted, advertising, because it is an infrastructure of the industrial system, also exhibits the features and characteristics of the latter. Industrial bigness calls for giant advertising agencies with impressive billings and facilities to handle large accounts. In examining the agency billings for 1971 (both U.S. and foreign), one is struck with the extent and level of concentration. The giant agencies—such as J. Walter Thompson, McCann-Erickson, Ted Bates and Co.—are the recipients of the benefits of direct foreign investment and of the expansion of the world consumer system. With total 1971 billings of $774 million, J. Walter Thompson is a far-flung empire; McCann-Erickson is a viable second with $593.9 million.

The 1971 annual survey of *Advertising Age* (in the March 1972 issue) reported a total number of 1,366 agencies in 76 countries with total billings of $16.9 billion. A quick computation done for the benefit of this analysis, revealed that slightly less than 1% of the agencies were responsible for 31% of the billings.

Much of the effort behind advertising and product differentiation seems wasteful and highly conducive to industrial concentration because of the undue advantage conferred upon the giants. Furthermore, the relative ease with which the multinational giants can dominate the world communication system, seems to undermine the free flow of information and unjustly give a small number of individuals and organizations a near-monopoly on what should be viewed as a genuinely global resource.

HIGH ENTRY BARRIERS

The last cost of oligopoly to be briefly treated here is the question of entry barriers. Though I will employ its standard and conventional usage—the relative ease or difficulty with which a new competitor can enter a particular market—I am principally concerned with the ability of non-Western firms to enter markets controlled by giant multinationals. Quite recently, the Committee on Manufactures of the UN Conference on Trade and Development (1971) has given some thought to this problem. In focusing on restrictive business practices that affect the ability of firms in non-Western countries to successfully enter and compete in the world economy, the activities of the multinationals were briefly examined. Vertically integrated multinationals, the committee concluded, tend to preclude export activities on the part of underdeveloped firms. The multinationals generally tend to be self-sufficient, and the opportunities are not as abundant as they should be for non-Western firms to engage in auxiliary activities such as supplying, servicing, and so forth.

The gravity of this problem cannot be overstated, nor could the difficulties that non-Western companies are likely to encounter. Witness the difficulty that some of the giants themselves have had in trying to enter the international computer market, for example. Dominated by IBM, which controls 70% of the American market, 73% of Germany's, 50% of Britain's, 74% of France's, 40% of Japan's (but 60% by value of sales), and 80% of Italy's (Harmon, 1971: 19), the computer market seems to be characterized by an extremely high entry barrier. Both RCA and GE found it impossible to make significant inroads into it. With IBM controlling computer hardware, software, peripheral equipment, and support services, the possibility of even entering the market at the periphery is quite slim. Most observers also concede the difficulty of a major entry into the world automotive industry. A tight financial system, the difficulty of generating the capital required, and the marketing system which the industry has structured make a major challenge highly improbable. High entry barriers to oligopolistic industries perpetuate inefficiency, prevent the entry of new competitive forces, and help create a general atmosphere of stagnation.

Conclusion: The Multinationals as Oligopolists

Focusing attention on the problems that oligopoly raises for world consumers and linking worldwide concentration with

multinational corporate activity help steer the debate about the
multinationals toward more fruitful and crucial endeavors. At
issue are such urgent questions as the impacts and costs visited
upon us all by powerful, large firms whose powers are neither
checked nor adequately defined. Putting before us what is
flashy and appealing, as well as what is essential, multinational
giants help shape the world in which we live, yet elementary
knowledge about the ways in which they do so is still lacking.

Particularly pressing and important in this context is not only
the search for remedies to corporate oligopoly and giantism, but
the quest for alternative visions and models of what a proper
economic order looks like. The search would free us from the
inhibiting constraints of what is and demonstrate to us the
possibilities of reform, and, more importantly, of fundamental
change. Otherwise, we would be imprisoned by our own sense
of futility and resignation, dissatisfied with the world of the
oligopolists, but unable to advance any meaningful and viable
alternatives.

REFERENCES

ADELMAN, M. A. (1970) "The two faces of economic concentration." Public
   Interest 21 (Fall): 117-126.
BAIN, J. S. (1966) International Differences in Industrial Structure. New Haven,
   Conn.: Yale Univ. Press.
BARAN, P. and P. SWEEZY (1966) Monopoly and Capital. New York: Monthly
   Review Press.
BARBER, R. J. (1970) The American Corporation: Its Power, Its Money, Its Politics.
   New York: E. P. Dutton.
BERG, A. (1972) "Industry's struggle with world malnutrition." Harvard Business
   Rev. 50 (January/February): 130-141.
BORGSTROM, G. (1967) The Hungry Planet: The Modern World at the Edge of
   Famine. New York: Macmillan.
COMANOR, W. and T. WILSON (1969) "Advertising and the advantages of size."
   Amer. Economic Rev. 59 (May): 87-98.
DRUCKER, P. (1969) The Age of Discontinuity. New York: Harper & Row.
GALBRAITH, J. K. (1967) The New Industrial State. Boston: Houghton Mifflin.
GREEN, M. J. [ed.] (1971) "The closed enterprise system." Nader Study Group
   Report on Antitrust Enforcement. Washington, D.C.: Center for the Study of
   Responsive Law.
HARMON, A. (1971) The International Computer Industry. Cambridge, Mass.:
   Harvard Univ. Press.

HELLMAN, R. (1970) The Challenge to U.S. Dominance of the International Corporation. New York: Dunellen.
HYMER, S. (1970) "The efficiency (contradictions) of multinational corporations." Amer. Economic Rev. 60 (May): 441-448.
McGEE, J. S. (1971) In Defense of Industrial Concentration. New York: Praeger.
MODELSKI, G. (1971) "Multinational business: a global perspective." Presented at the One Hundred Thirty-Ninth Meeting of the American Association for the Advancement of Science, Philadelphia, December.
OZAWA, T. (1971) "Transfer of technology from Japan to developing countries." UNITAR Research Report 7, New York.
PENROSE, E. (1968) The Large International Firm in Developing Countries. Cambridge, Mass.: MIT Press.
PERLMUTTER, H. (1969) "Some management problems in spaceship earth: the megafirm and the global industrial estate." Academy of Management Proceedings: 59-93.
——— (1968) "Supergiant firms of the future." Wharton Q. (Winter): 8-14.
QUINN, J. (1969) "Technology transfer by multinational companies." Harvard Business Rev. 47 (November/December): 147-161.
REDDAWAY, W. B. (1967) Effects of U.K. Direct Investment Overseas. Cambridge, Eng.: Cambridge Univ. Press.
ROWTHORN, R. with S. HYMER (1971) International Big Business 1957-1967: A Study of Comparative Growth. Cambridge, Eng.: Cambridge Univ. Press.
SCHERER, F. M. (1970) Industrial Market Structure and Economic Performance. Chicago: Rand McNally.
——— (1965) "Firm size, market structure, opportunity, and the output of patented inventions." Amer. Economic Rev. 55 (December): 1097-1125.
SCHILLER, H. (1971) "Madison Avenue imperialism." Trans-action (March/April): 52-58, 64.
SCHUMPETER, J. (1942) Capitalism, Socialism and Democracy. New York: Harper & Row.
SHEPHERD, W. F. (1970) Market Power and Economic Welfare. New York: Random House.
SUTTON, F. et al. (1962) The American Business Creed. New York: Schocken.
SWANN, D. and D. L. McLACHLAN (1967) Concentration or Competition: A European Dilemma. London: Chatham House.
TANZER, M. (1969) The Political Economy of International Oil and the Under-developed Countries. Boston: Beacon.
Task Force on the Structure of Canadian Industry (1968) Foreign Ownership and the Structure of Canadian Industry. Ottawa: Queen's Printer.
United Nations Conference on Trade and Development Committee on Manufactures (1971) Restrictive Business Practices (TD/B/c.2/104 and TD/122/supp. 1). New York.
U.S. Cabinet Task Force on Oil Import Control (1970) The Oil Import Question. Washington, D.C.
VERNON, R. (1971) Sovereignty at Bay: The Multinational Spread of U.S. Enterprises. New York: Basic Books.
WATSON, D. and M. HOLMAN (1967) "Concentration of patents from government-financed research in industry." Rev. of Economics and Statistics 49 (August): 375-381.

Marx, Universalism, and Contemporary World Business

FRIEDRICH VON KROSIGK
German Science Foundation

In placing the multinational corporation into the scope of international politics, contemporary students of international relations are venturing into a field which, until recently, was still considered the privileged domain of Marxist-oriented scholars. The approach to world politics in the West having received its particular shape from the preoccupation with traditional political, legal, and military questions tended to ignore economic perspectives regarding them as Marxist heresy. The new emphasis currently placed on the political aspects of multinational business operations seems to correct this narrow view. The critical confrontation with the Marxist approach to international politics, however, is lagging behind.

Whenever Marxist thought is taken into consideration in the debate on multinational business, it remains limited to reflections on Lenin's theory of imperialism which, though an important element, is not the entire story of the Marxist contribution to the study of international relations. Surprisingly, Marx himself, as initiator of the political theory and analysis of economic entities in international politics, is passed over in silence.

In the following pages, we draw attention to the continuity of a process of reflection which connects the early Marxist tradition of political thought with recent efforts to evaluate the impact of the multinational corporation on the international system. Our point of departure is the discussion of Marx's original approach to international politics with special regard to the function and role he attributed to the capitalist enterprise as international actor. This excursion to the beginnings of the revolutionary theory of international relations will be contrasted with the more influential Leninist revision in order to show how current debates in some way actually mirror differences of approach and issues already familiar to students of Marxism.

Marxian Universalism

Marx is known above all as a sharp critic of nineteenth-century European capitalism. But in order to understand Marx as a revolutionary observer of international politics, it is necessary to add to this common cliché that he was also a great admirer of the spectacular eruption of economic and technological progress shaking Europe in the sway of the Industrial Revolution. No liberal apologist of the Industrial Revolution can match the enthusiasm which Marx displayed in the Communist Manifesto in describing the achievements of the bourgeoisie in this epoch:

> The bourgeoisie, during its rule of scarcely one hundred years, has created more massive and more colossal productive forces than have all preceding generations together. The subjection of nature's forces to man and machinery, the application of chemistry to industry and agriculture, steam-navigation, railways and electric telegraphs, the clearing of whole continents for cultivation, the canalization of rivers and the conjuring of whole populations out of the ground—what earlier century had even a presentiment that such productive forces slumbered in the lap of social labor? [Marx and Engels, 1847: 17-18].

It is against this background of the Industrial Revolution and its particularly "progressive" reception in Marxian thought that we are better able to recognize a conception of international politics that shifts emphasis from traditional political actors to economic forces and that is centered squarely upon the concept of production. Whether Marx addressed the domestic or international scene of politics, he started from the assumption that the labor process determines the totality of human existence[1] and thus gives to society—whether national or international in scope—its elementary pattern. In unfolding the dynamics of the labor process, Marx unfolded the problem of social as well as interstate relations. Being drawn into the whirlpool of industry and production, man and the entire world surrounding him were losing their natural persistence and stability: "the world surrounding us is not something given and the same for all eternity but the product of industry and of the state of society in the sense that it is a historical product" (Marx and Engels, 1846: 417).

In simplified terms, the Marxian world received its particular dynamic from a persistent tension between a sweeping expansion of the material forces of production and stagnating relations of production resulting in antagonistic property arrangements which finally explode periodically into open class conflict. "The history of all hitherto existing society is the history of class-struggle," Marx proclaimed in the opening passages of the Communist Manifesto. Classes, instead of traditional political actors such as nations or states, appeared as dominant historical forces; and class conflict, instead of interstate conflict, occupied the center of attention. Integrated in the historical dynamic of productive forces and class conflict, the nation-state emerged in Marx's theory as the political superstructure of the capitalist process of production. Capitalism had centralized population and industry and concentrated property in a few hands, thus creating the conditions and "need" for political centralization: "Independent, or but loosely connected, provinces with separate interests, laws, governments and systems of taxation, had to be lumped together into one nation, with one government, one code of

---

1. See Marx's (1844) discussion of the problem of labor with regard to Hegel's phenomenology in the economic and philosophic manuscripts.

laws, one national class-interest, one frontier and one customs-tariff" (Marx and Engels, 1847: 17). Geared to the specific structure of capitalist production, the nation-state functioned as the managing committee of the ruling class; the bourgeoisie acted internally to maintain the system of exploitation and externally to assist the internationally expanding capitalist enterprise in conquering new markets.

The cumulative, expansive nature of capitalist production was the connecting link between domestic and international politics; consequently, both realms of politics were closely interwoven. Both had the same structural basis of conflict:

> To the extent that the exploitation of one individual by another is put to an end, the exploitation of one nation by another will also be put to an end. To the extent that the antagonism within the nation vanishes the hostility of one nation to another will come to an end [Marx and Engels, 1847: 31].

Both reflected in their different patterns the specific state of development of the process of production on which they were structurally dependent: "The relations of various nations with one another depend upon the extent to which each of them has developed its productive forces, the division of labor and domestic commerce" (Marx and Engels, 1846: 410).

In tracing the expansive logic of the capitalist system of production, Marx discovered the dynamics of an international system in transition from competitive national confrontation to global cooperation. Capitalism unified the nation-state only to declare the transcendence of the nation-state and the emergence of international relations on a truly global scale. Classic Marxist internationalism was the revolutionary companion of nineteenth-century liberal free trade ideology, heralding the decline of international strife in the wake of growing commercial interdependence. Though, for Marx, a truly nonantagonistic international order was ultimately dependent on the dissolution of class-conflict, growing commercial integration, too, was considered to be a factor of lessening interstate conflict. Unlike the later Lenin and unlike contemporary, radical ideology, Marx did not claim a causal relationship between international expansion of capitalism and war except for the formative phase of capitalist accumulation. Here, he admitted, "With the rise of manufacturing the various nations entered into a competitive relationship, the competition for trade was fought out in wars, protective duties and prohibitions" (Marx and Engels, 1846: 448). But as soon as Marx turned to the spectacle of mature capitalism—capitalism embracing big industry, free trade, a world market, and universalized competition—he designed an international scene where national differences and interstate conflict are visibly in decline:

> National differences and antagonism are daily more and more vanishing, owing to the development of the bourgeoisie, to freedom of commerce, to the world market, to uniformity in the mode of production and in the conditions of life corresponding thereto [Marx and Engels, 1847: 30].

The integration of the capitalist nations into the world market inaugurated the formation of a world society. With production and consumption becoming increasingly cosmopolitan in character, the national ground was being drawn from under the feet of industry and, "in place of the old local and national seclusion and self-sufficiency we have intercourse in every direction, a universal interdependence of nations. . . . National one-sidedness and narrow-mindedness become more and more impossible" (Marx and Engels, 1847: 17). Formerly competing nations were growing together under the imperatives of a universalized division of labor instituting "all-around dependence" and "world historical co-operation" (Marx and Engels, 1846: 430).

In Marx's view, the revolutionary function of the expanding capitalist enterprise was twofold: to create the material base for a cooperative global system, and to act as catalyst of social conflict. The "heavy artillery" of cheap capitalist commodities not only "batters down all Chinese walls"—i.e., national boundaries—it also induces social conflict on a global scale, thus contributing to the formation of a global proletariat. In 1848, Marx assumed that the European proletariat had already outgrown national boundaries. "The working men have no country," he proclaimed. "We cannot take from them what

they have not got" (Marx and Engels, 184\
continuing international expansion of capitalism,
this trend to extend into other continents, ?
particular countries under colonial rule, and h
condemn this trend in terms typical for today's Marxi:
attitude toward the "British rule in India" may se.   ..s an
illustration of this point.

Marx (1853: 475) certainly did not have any tender feelings
for the British colonial system in India. "There cannot . . .
remain any doubt, but that the misery inflicted by the British
on Hindustan is of an essentially different and infinitely more
intensive kind than all Hindustan had to suffer before." But, as
would be nowadays popular, he did not attack the British
"rule" for violating the sacred right to national self-
determination. Instead, he weighed the criminal aspect of
colonialism against its universal revolutionary consequences and
finally concluded in favor of the latter:

> England, it is true, in causing a social revolution in Hindustan, was
> actuated only by the vilest interests, and was stupid in her manner of
> enforcing them. But that is not the question. The question is: Can
> mankind fulfill its destiny without a fundamental revolution in the
> social state of Asia? If not, whatever may have been the crimes of
> England, she was the unconscious tool of history in bringing about that
> revolution [Marx, 1853: 481].

The same revolutionary internationalism was guiding Marx
when he supported the case of free trade in the mid-nineteenth-
century quarrel between protectionists and free-traders. Not
that he expected free trade to offer more humane economic
conditions than a protectionist customs union would. But by
accelerating the corrosion of the nation-state, Marx believed the
free-trade system would ultimately speed up the social revolution, thus justifying the greater violence it imposed on the
working class.[2]

2. The relevant texts on the free trade issue are: K. Marx: Die Schutzzöllner, die
Freihandelsmänner und die arbeitende Klasse, pp. 296-298 in MEGA (Marx-Engels
Gesamtausgabe, Dietz Verlag Berlin, 1963) IV. F. Engels: Der Freihandelskongress in
Brussel, pp. 299-308 in MEGA IV. K. Marx: Rede über die Frage des Freihandels, pp.
444-458 in MEGA IV.

Marx's confidence in the corrosive force of an internationally expanding capitalism received its most eloquent expression in his conception of revolution. Only a society which is in possession of globally expanding productive forces, existing, therefore, "on a world-historical rather than a local scale" could be considered mature for a communist revolution. The revolution itself was designed as universal as its economic basis. Marx expected it to involve simultaneously at least "the leading civilized countries," such as Britain, America, France, and Germany.[3] "Empirically, communism is only possible as the act of dominant peoples, 'all at once' and simultaneously which presupposes the universal development of productive power and world wide interaction linked with communism" (Marx and Engels, 1846: 427).

Of course, Marx was aware that preceding this universal eruption the proletariat would have to gain supremacy within its own national surroundings, and he admitted that "though not in substance, yet in form, the struggle of the proletariat with the bourgeoisie is at first a national struggle" (Marx and Engels, 1847: 30).[4]

For strategic reasons Marx continued to count on the nation-state, and increasingly so, the more he experienced its stubborn reality in nineteenth-century Europe's life. But from a theoretical point of view, he remained convinced that the bourgeois institution of the nation-state had outlived itself. The "heavy artillery" of capitalist enterprise having advanced beyond its protective national boundaries and taken position in the world market also paved the way beyond the nation-state.

3. P. 374 in MEGA V.
4. There is no doubt that the more Marx gets involved in practical politics, the more his emphasis shifts from "substance" to "form" in the revolutionary struggle–i.e., national independence gradually turns into a revolutionary ideal. See Marx and Engel's engagement for national independence of Poland, pp. 319-363 in MEGA V; Hungary, pp. 165-187 in MEGA VI; Ireland, pp. 376 and 398-400 in MEGA XXXI. However, the theoretical consequences of this shift of perspective have never been elaborated. See also Marx's dispute with Lassalle on communist internationalism in "Critique of the Gotha Program": "The internationalism of the program (Lassalle's Gotha Program) stands even infinitely below that of the Free Trade Party," Marx contends, because it does not take into account "the international functions of the German working class" within the framework of the world market and the global system of states.

Convinced that one could not foresee the postrevolutionary future, Marx speculated little about the structure of this global community which the communist revolution was supposed to transfer into actuality. His idea of a "world-historical co-operation of individuals" remained as vague as the idea of the future communist society in general (Marx and Engels, 1846: 425-430). And even Engels' renowned passage "from government of men to the administration of things," an idea in his Anti-Dühring borrowed from Saint-Simon, contributed little to make communism more concrete. But it seems certain that Marxian thought has no room for the postulate of an "absolute unity of mankind," as Berki (1971: 80) wants to see it. Nor does Marx vacillate between two positions in regard to the future of human society: "complete unity" and "non-antagonistic diversity along national lines" (Berki, 1971: 86). Whenever he vacillates, it is between theory and praxis. The nation-state coincides, according to Marx, with capitalism and will "wither away" with capitalism. But diversity is not the privilege of the nation-state system. There are more things on earth than national diversity, especially for Marx, the apologist for the Paris Commune.

The fate of the Marxian revolution is well known. Its failure—no communist revolution occurred under conditions and according to patterns defined by Marx— has stimulated a more skeptical evaluation of the corrosive, revolutionary effect of the international expansion of capitalism. The post-Marxian revolutionary discussion in fact produced a radical shift of perspective in favor of the nation-state as focus of revolutionary activity. Marxists engaged themselves in the struggle for "national autonomy." The increasing internationalization of capitalism acquired a new attribute of threat. In his preface to the Polish (1892) and Italian (1893) editions of the Communist Manifesto, Engels already placed the struggle for "national autonomy" into the very center of revolutionary activity and national self-determination; what for Marx was an obsolete notion, now became a revolutionary ideal. "Die Wiederherstellung eines unabhängigen starken Polens," he wrote, "ist aber eine Sache, die nicht nur die Polen, sondern die uns alle angeht. Ein aufrichtiges internationales Zusammenwirken der europäischen Nationen ist nur möglich, wenn jede dieser Nationen im eigenen Hause vollkommen ist."[5] The "proletarian age," the beginning of which Engels jubilantly announced, became the age of the nation-state and patriotism, for Marx a repellent bourgeois ideal. Lenin's tactical move toward "socialism in one country"—though conceived as "spark" of a global revolution—sealed the all too optimistic chapter of Marxian universalism.

Leninist Imperialism

It is in the framework of a theory of imperialism, as developed with various modifications by Hobson, Hilferding, Bukharin, Rosa Luxemburg, and Lenin, that the Marxist tradition has received the conceptual tools to cope with the more critical aspects of the internationalization of capitalism which Marx had not anticipated. In particular in its influential Leninist shape, this theory is designed to explain the striking contradictions of an international system in which, contrary to Marxian predictions, progressing international economic relations were coexisting with an increasing polarization of nation-states and growing international violence.

Writing his "Imperialism" on the eve of the Russian Revolution and under the direct impact of World War I, Lenin did not lack pressing reasons for integrating the category of interstate conflict into the revolutionary theory of international relations. Structural modifications in the capitalist economy are his key arguments in charging the capitalist enterprise with a new "rationale" as catalyst of international violence.[6]

Marx had based his revolutionary theory of international politics on a competitive model derived from the study of mid-nineteenth-century operations of capitalism in Europe.

5. P. 588 in MEGA IV.
6. We are briefly discussing this shift of perspective in Marxist thought without ambition to present a comprehensive analysis of the theory of imperialism. Our focus is on the new "rationale" which the capitalist enterprise receives in this context, and we are limiting our scope to the Leninist version of imperialism.

Lenin faced a new world of industrial and financial monopolies in which the "natural law" of free competition was passing away. The great industrial combine and financial associations which emerged as power centers of the capitalist economy in the last quarter of the nineteenth century were strong enough to suppress self-destructive competition and ensure stable profit levels regardless of market conditions. This movement of concentration, simultaneously, was backed by a movement of international expansion for which the export of capital as distinguished from the traditional export of commodities acquired exceptional importance.[7] It is this monopolistic and at the same time intensified expansive element in capitalism—both anticipated by Marx but not in this form and not as a stable and essential element of capitalism—which provided the economic base for Lenin's struggle with a new type of political reality in which imperialism and nationalism became the dominant features.[8]

The trend toward imperialism, the mad scramble for colonial acquisition in which most European industrial states were involved by the end of the nineteenth century was for Lenin, following Hobson's (1902) guide, only the logical consequence of capitalism entering the stage of monopoly. It is this linkage between monopoly capital and colonial exploitation which, Lenin argued, explained both the unexpected strength of the capitalist enterprise and its specific contribution to international violence.

"Super-profits" gained from colonial exploitation were used to counteract Marx's law of falling profits in highly developed economies as well as to bribe certain important segments of the proletariat. Social polarization and impoverishment, the twin preludes to Marxian revolution, however missing in Europe, could in this way be effectively undermined. While exploitation intensified in the colonial world, an opportunistic "labor aristocracy," sharing colonial super-profits, formed in the

---

7. "Typical of the old capitalism, when free competition held undivided sway, was the export of goods. Typical of the latest stage of capitalism, when monopolies rule, is the export of capital" (Lenin, 1961: 127).

8. See chapters 4, 23, 24 of Kapital in MEGA XXIII.

industrialized countries and blocked the road to world revolution.[9] Bribery and opportunism were Lenin's key arguments in dealing with the problem of the patriotism of Europe's working men, who rallied in 1914 to their respective flags though they were supposed to "have no country."

In revising Marx to fit the new world of monopolies and colonial exploitation, Lenin sketched a conception of world politics in which the relationships which Marx tried to develop between internationalization of capitalism, growing interdependence and decreasing international conflict was, finally, converted into a correlation of capitalism and war: "Imperial wars are absolutely inevitable . . . as long as private property in the means of production exists" (Lenin, 1916: 113). Violent conflict was institutionalized in this revised Marxist theory of international relations on two different levels. On the one hand, there is the overall class conflict between advanced capitalist (or bourgeois) and underdeveloped colonial (or proletarian) countries in which the Marxian scheme of class struggle, with its implications of impoverishment and polarization, is reproduced on a gigantic international scale: "Capitalism has grown into a world system of colonial oppression and of the financial strangulation of the overwhelming majority of the world by a handful of 'advanced' countries" (Lenin, 1916: 113).

On the other hand, there is a new level of international conflict resulting from competition among capitalist countries struggling for territorial and market hegemony. World War I served as Lenin's illustration of this type of international violence, and, in his perspective, this was "a war to decide whether the British or German group of financial plunderers is to receive the most booty" (Lenin, 1916: 114).

Though Lenin recognized that, under the impact of increasing international capital movements, "things 'naturally' gravitated . . . towards the formation of international cartels" (1916: 130), he did not believe this transnational trend of capitalism to have a harmonizing effect on the relations among

9. "Imperialism . . . makes it economically possible to bribe the upper strata of the proletariat and thereby fosters . . . opportunism" (Lenin, 1916: 143).

capitalist countries.[10] His unconvincingly explained assumption is that competition shifts at the stage of monopoly capitalism from the firms to the national level. The political role of the capitalist enterprise converges with that of the nation-state. Its extended political power corresponds to an extended global system of exploitation in which the potential of revolution turns away from Europe, where Marx had placed it, to the neo-proletarian, backward regions.

The divergent conclusions at which Marx and Lenin arrived in evaluating the role of the capitalist enterprise as international actor are the expression of different historical experiences as well as of different perspectives and approaches. While both recognized the expansive element inherent in the capitalist mode of production, they each emphasized different aspects and consequences. Marx' focus was on the universal cooperative potential in the capitalist drive beyond national boundaries. When he welcomed free trade or even colonial expansion, he was attracted by the promise of an emergent cosmopolitan order, with universalized communication and global inter-dependence as material bases of a future cooperative world society. Since, for Marx, the nation-state and capitalism were coexistent, the venture of the capitalist enterprise beyond national boundaries by itself assumed revolutionary significance.

Lenin above all drew attention to the new dimensions of power and conflict which had become manifest in the course of the international expansion of capitalism. In particular, he corrected Marx by showing that internationalization of capitalism and the consolidation of the nation-state did not contradict each other at all. The happy marriage of political nationalism and economic internationalism appeared to him as the secret of imperialism. Lenin turned to the nation-state as the new base of revolutionary struggle because, in his experience, the internationalization of capitalism neither diminished international

10. See Lenin's controversy with Kautzky on this subject (Lenin, 1916: 130-131). Kautzky developed a conception of "ultra-imperialism" which envisaged collective exploitation of the world by a united international finance capital replacing the traditional rivalries of national finance capital.

conflict nor eroded national boundaries. Unfortunately, Lenin never worked out the theoretical consequences of this non-Marxian situation. Marx derived his revolutionary theory, as we said, from a competitive model of capitalism in which monopolistic dimensions of power, though visible, were not the essential elements. Lenin merely stretched this model with the tools of "bribery" and "opportunism" instead of exploring the working principles and "laws of motion" of the new world of capitalism under conditions of monopoly, nationalism and imperial wars (Baran and Sweezy, 1966: 5).

However, the purpose of this paper is not to confirm or to refute Lenin or Marx but to draw both into confrontation with the contemporary challenge of multinational business. In tracing the revolutionary critique of the capitalist enterprise as international actor, we have acquired the theoretical base from which we can proceed in this direction. In the following pages, we attempt to show the Marxian and the Leninist dimensions in the present theory and praxis of the multinational corporation.

The Marxian and the Leninist Imperatives Reviewed

Since Marx discovered that it is in the nature of capitalism to enmesh "all the peoples of the world . . . in the net of the world market"[11] and Lenin noticed that large-scale financial and industrial enterprises had moved into the focus of world politics, the internationalization and concentration of economic forces has rapidly gained momentum. Trade and financial operations, still the major dimensions of capitalist internationalization for Marx and Lenin, are being surpassed, today, by a wave of international production. The multinational corporation, in its predominant role as transfer agent of productive factors, is becoming the principal actor of the world economy. This trend is supported by a movement of concentration in face of which the now often-repeated vision (Barber, 1970: 264) of a global economy controlled by perhaps 200 or 300 giant

11. See p. 790 in MEGA XXXIII.

corporations is losing its utopian connotation. In 1916, Lenin still could charge that 3,000 giant enterprises were controlling 50% of the total U.S. production. Today he would have to correct these figures in favor of approximately 200 firms (Barber, 1970: 20-21).

Both the power and the size of the modern large-scale corporation have assumed dimensions which do not favor the Leninist forecast that capitalism is on the road of "stagnation and decay." On the contrary, mergers, industrial diversification, and internationalization, the dimensions of recent corporate expansion, indicate a degree of organizational flexibility, territorial independence, and financial strength that only mean greater long-range stability. Nor has the present wave of international expansion of corporations from bases in the United States, Europe, and Japan aroused any revolutionary enthusiasm. Europe's communist parties prefer to support a defensive Gaullist strategy of national strength and independence in battling the "American challenge,"[12] even while classic Marxian internationalism has become the characteristic of admirers of the multinational corporation. The conflicting views of Marx and Lenin with regard to the challenge of internationalization of capitalism are surprisingly revived in the present confrontation between admirers and critics of the multinational corporation.

When George Ball (1967: 80), reflects that "the nation-state is a very old fashioned idea and badly adapted to serve the needs of our present complex world" and Kindleberger (1969: 207) contends in the same mood that "the nation-state is just about through as an economic unit," they both seem to echo the optimistic internationalism of the Communist Manifesto despite their ideological distance from Marx and Engels; both seem to share with classic Marxism a strong dose of technological and economic determinism, which the history of capitalism during the past hundred years has decisively refuted.

Yet the disjunction between the world economy and the

12. See also Bell (1971), who contends that contemporary revolutionary movements are basically nationalist in scope.

nation-state in which the Communist Manifesto detected a springboard for global revolutionary transformations has hardly disappeared. The fact that today a corporation like Standard Oil of New Jersey operates in scores of countries and derives more than half its income or earnings from "foreign" sales is still a demonstration of both economic globalization and American enterprise, but no proof that the nation-state is in decline. Behrman's (1971: 13) calculation that, if current growth rates and foreign investment trends continue at the same pace, by 1990 nearly 70% of the noncommunist world's gross product may be owned, controlled, or financed by United States-based companies indicates the new imperial potential of power and control burdening the "promise" of the multinational corporation. As long as ownership and control of the multinational corporation remain located in one nation, the often celebrated "innovative" qualities of multinationality can hardly raise excitement outside the world of business. In fact, they raise the question whether such corporations are at all multinational.

Waltz (1970) has well marked the critical connection between decentralization of operations, as practiced by multinational corporations, and centralization of control which apologists of global interdependence tend to pass over in silence. However, he misses the point when he infers from the dominant position of American-controlled business a general decline of interdependence. Since Hegel (1807: 141-150), we know that the relationship of master and slave tightly combines interdependence and inequality. The basic question today is whether the rise of the multinational corporation merely opens a new version of a recurrent Hegelian master-slave dialectic or holds out the prospects of a nonantagonistic world order.

The most forceful argument in favor of the multinational corporation as a factor of international stability and peace could be the postwar experience of developed Western nations. The strong position of American and European multinational firms within the Common Market indicates that their activity has on the whole fostered and reinforced the trend toward integration among European countries. It is difficult to deny, however, that this apparent harmony of the Western "business community" is in the long run overshadowed by the political and social implications of American predominance and superiority and burdened with the prospects of an international order in which the prosperity and peace of a few highly industrialized nations are achieved on the basis of an increasing pauperization of a major part of the world population. While, as Modelski (1971) points out, the causal relationship between capitalist economic expansion and war, which Lenin postulated, is not verifiable as a general rule, it seems more difficult to reject the claims of a nonquantifiable, structural connection between corporate expansion and international violence,[13] which is coming to the fore in recent theories of neocolonialism or neo-imperialism (Frank, 1967; Magdoff, 1969; Horowitz, 1969a, 1969b; Galtung, 1971; Sunkel, 1972; see also Fanon, 1968; Julien, 1968; Riencourt, 1968; Jallée, 1970; Ackerman and Kindleberger, 1971). Accordingly, the direct military and political presence of imperial powers rather than a specific pattern of trade and investment relations is considered responsible for the growing "strangulation" of the Third World and the widening gap between rich industrial and poor developing nations. As Galtung (1971: 91) puts it: "Only imperfect, amateurish imperialism needs weapons: professional imperialism is based on structural rather than direct violence."

Radicalizing the Leninist idea of a "labor aristocracy"[14] assumed to function as a bridgehead of capitalist interest across national boundaries, this conception of neo-imperialism views the multinational corporation as the driving force of a sophisticated global system of dominance in which backward regions are "peacefully" attached to industrial core-areas as the result of their progressing economic dependence and inferiority. It is this configuration of global interpenetration and centralization of power which inspires Hymer's (1972: 114) sobering predictions about the implications of multinational business for the international system.

13. For an exploration of the concept of structural violence, see Galtung (1969).
14. Quoting Engels, Lenin (1916: 145) writes about the English proletariat: "the workers gaily share the feast of England's monopoly of the world market and the colonies." See also Galtung (1971: 112, n. 4).

Hymer's vision of a "new imperial system" receives support from recent assessments indicating that the activity of the multinational corporation so far has heavily concentrated in the industrial core areas of North America, Western Europe, and Japan. It is looming behind the now widely noticed imbalance between rich and poor countries (Modelski, 1970a; Runnalls, 1971). It is contradicted, however, by an outburst of corporate conscience in favor of global responsibilities (Ball, 1967; Tannenbaum, 1968; Ford, 1971; Hobbing, 1971).

The multinational corporation as "road to peace and prosperity" (Ford, 1971) appears in the role of a "genuine vehicle of international co-operation" with "respect to the human condition;" it is committed to "the people of the World, not the people of any one nation or of any political ideology," and more devoted to fighting world poverty than was Karl Marx, who just "wanted to strip the bourgeoisie of its increasing power and ... had no notion that poverty could be ended" (Hobbing, 1971: 46). If there is anything substantial about these claims, they should become visible among others in the statistics of international investment, production, trade, and consumption in favor of the Third World.

When more than a century ago, Marx (1844: 304) observed the expansion of the capitalist enterprise beyond the nation-state, he anticipated the prelude to global revolutionary transformations ultimately leading mankind from its "prehistory" of violence into a truly "human" history—i.e., a history not of affluence but of reconciliation between "man and nature and man and man." Today it would be naive to connect similar expectations with the new business expansion into the international realm. The general fate of the Marxian revolution as well as the new potentials of "imperial" control are well suited to sober revolutionary speculations. In contrasting Marxian universalism and Leninist imperialism, we have revealed the dialectic of promise and threat that limits the corrosive power of the capitalist enterprise as an international actor.

If any hope can be attached to the multinational corporation, it would have to point modestly in the direction of a movement toward greater international responsibility bringing the global structure of the multinational corporation into harmony with a global mechanism of control. Contemporary observers of international business (Vernon, 1971: 272) tend to consider such reflections as "out of joint with the times." In Marxist perspective, a step toward "true" internationalization of the multinational corporation would come close to the end of capitalism and thus appear even more utopian. As Sweezy (and Magdoff, 1969: 9) states, "To exist, capital must have nationality. If, for example, the state of the nation to which it belonged were to collapse, capital would lose its indispensible protector." It remains to be seen whether this is the last word on this important subject.

REFERENCES

ACKERMAN, F. and C. KINDLEBERGER (1971) "Magdoff on imperialism." Public Policy (Summer): 525-534.

BALL, G. (1967) "The promise of the multinational corporation." Fortune 75 (June 1): 80.

BARAN, P. and P. SWEEZY (1966a) Monopoly Capital. New York: Monthly Review Press.

——— (1966b) "Notes on the theory of imperialism," in Problems of Economic Dynamics and Planning. Oxford: Pergamon.

BARBER, F. J. (1970) The American Corporation. New York: E. P. Dutton.

BEHRMAN, J. N. (1971) "New orientation in international trade and investment," in P. Uri (ed.) Trade and Investment Policies for the Seventies. New York: Praeger.

——— (1970) National Interests and the Multinational Enterprise. Englewood Cliffs, N.J.: Prentice-Hall.

BELL, J. B. (1971) "Contemporary revolutionary organizations." International Organization 25 (Autumn): 503-518.

BERKI, R. N. (1971) "On Marxian thought and the problem of international relations." World Politics 24 (October): 81-105.

CROZIER, M. (1969) "A new rationale for American business." Daedalus: Perspectives on Business 98 (Winter): 147-158.

FANON, F. (1968) The Wretched of the Earth. New York: Grove.

FORD, H. (1971) "Multinationalism: road to peace and prosperity." Public Relations Q. 15 (Winter): 9-10, 26.

FRANK, A. G. (1967) Capitalism and Underdevelopment in Latin America. New York: Monthly Review Press.

GALBRAITH, J. K. (1967) The New Industrial State. Boston: Houghton Mifflin.

GALTUNG, J. (1971) "A structural theory of imperialism." J. of Peace Research 8, 2: 82-117.

——— (1969) "Violence, peace and peace research." J. of Peace Research 6: 67-91.

HEGEL, G.W.F. (1807) Phanomenologie des Geistes. Hamburg: Meiner Verlag.

HOBBING, E. (1971) "The world corporation: a catalytic agent?" Columbia J. of World Business 6 (July/August): 45-51.
HOBSON, J. A. (1902) Imperialism: A Study. London: Allen & Unwin.
HOROWITZ, D. [ed.] (1969a) Corporations and the Cold War. New York: Monthly Review Press.
——— (1969b) Empire and Revolution. New York: Random House.
HYMER, S. (1972) "The multinational corporation and the law of uneven development," in J. N. Bhagwati (ed.) Economics and World Order. New York: Macmillan.
JALLEE, P. (1970) The Pillage of the Third World. New York: Modern Reader.
JULIEN, U. (1968) L'Empire Americain. Paris: Grasset.
KINDLEBERGER, C. (1969) American Business Abroad. New Haven, Conn.: Yale Univ. Press.
LENIN, V. (1916) "Imperialism, the highest stage of capitalism," in E. Connor (ed.) Lenin on Politics and Revolution. New York: Pegasus.
MAGDOFF, H. (1969) The Age of Imperialism. New York: Monthly Review Press.
MARX, K. (1853) "The British rule in India," in E. Feuer (ed.) Basic Writings on Politics and Philosophy. New York: Doubleday Anchor.
——— (1844) "Economic and philosophic manuscripts," in D. Easton and M. Guddat (eds.) Writings of the Young Marx on Philosophy. New York: Doubleday Anchor.
——— and F. ENGELS (1847) The Communist Manifesto, in E. Feuer (ed.) Basic Writings on Politics and Philosophy. New York: Doubleday Anchor.
——— (1846) "The German ideology," in D. Easton and M. Guddat (eds.) Writings of the Young Marx on Philosophy. New York: Doubleday Anchor.
MASON, E. S. (1970) "The corporation in the post-industrial state." California Management Rev. 12 (Summer): 5-25.
MODELSKI, G. (1971) "Multinational business: a global perspective." Presented at the One Hundred Thirty-Ninth Meeting of the American Association for the Advancement of Science, Philadelphia, December.
——— (1970a) "Desarollo en el mundo." Folia Humanistica 8: 127-140.
——— (1970b) "The promise of geocentric politics." World Politics (July): 617-635.
POLK, J. (1968) "The new world economy." Columbia J. of World Business 3 (January/February): 7-15.
RIENCOURT, A. DE (1968) The American Empire. New York: Dial.
ROLFE, S. E. (1969) The International Corporation. Istanbul: International Chamber of Commerce.
RUNNALLS, J. D. (1971) The Widening Gap: Development in the 1970's. New York: Columbia Univ. Press.
SERVAN-SCHREIBER, J.-J. (1967) Le Défi Americain. Paris: Denoel.
SUNKEL, O. (1972) "Big business and 'dependencia.' " Foreign Affairs 50: 517-531.
SWEEZY, P. M. and H. MAGDOFF (1969) "Notes on the multinational corporation." Monthly Review 5, 6 (October, November): 1-7, 1-13.
TANNENBAUM, F. (1968) "The survival of the fittest." Columbia J. of World Business 3: 15-20.
VERNON, R. (1971) Sovereignty at Bay. New York: Basic Books.
WALTZ, K. (1970) "The myth of interdependence," in C. Kindleberger (ed.) The International Corporation. Cambridge, Mass.: MIT Press.

The Multinational Corporation

An Analytical Bibliography

FOUAD AJAMI
Department of Political Science
University of Washington

DAVID OSTERBERG
Peace and Conflict Programme
University of Lancaster

Given the proliferation of literature on the multinational corporation, any bibliographic survey is at best partial and incomplete. The task necessarily entailed some arbitrary and idiosyncratic choices, but it was also guided by a set of criteria that helped us approach a vast body of literature and select from it what we thought to be an adequate and representative sample. Our principal concern throughout was the potential utility of the product to what we conceived to be the clientele of this journal. In addition, we felt an obligation to include items that conveyed the various debates (both ideological and conceptual) surrounding the multinational corporation—its role in the world social system and in world order.

The following is a list of our inclusionary criteria and the items that were chosen when one or more of these criteria were applied:

(1) Several works qualified because they are statements by "influentials." Each academic subject seems to have an elite group which exercises influence, sets the tone and priorities of research, and provides the spark. This subject is no exception. Under this criterion, we included the entries by Vernon, Kindleberger, Hymer, Brown, and Perlmutter. The work by Rolfe and Damm also qualified here because the elites behind it are strategically placed in policy-making circles.

(2) Because the multinational corporation has provoked a good deal of ideological controversy, some works were included to convey the competing perspectives on the ideological spectrum. The entries by Magdoff and by Sweezy and Magdoff represent the thinking of some people on the left, and balance the views of business influentials and advocates. A liberal trend of thought seems to run through the works by Bell, Dahl, and Barber.

(3) The multinational corporation, we felt, is not only a question to be debated by academics, but one of considerable interest and importance to laymen and to an

attentive public. Thus it was important to include works by popularizers, and here the entries by Barber, Heilbroner, Jacoby, Turner, and Hellmann seemed appropriate.

(4) A number of works were chosen because they seemed to raise some broad theoretical questions with significant, though at first glance indirect, implications for those interested in the various facets of multinational enterprise. This criterion justifies the entries by Bell, Dahl, and Kapp.

(5) We tried to include works by social scientists, and, in particular, contributions by students of world politics. Here we chose Galloway, Wilkins, Lieberson, and the issue of *International Organization* edited by Keohane and Nye.

(6) Some data sources are listed because of their usefulness to those interested in conducting research on the multinationals. The entries by Judge and by Vaupel and Curhan qualified here.

(7) A large number of entries are related to issue areas or specific industries. The works by Guback, Jager, Levitt, Levy, Lieberson, Melman, Mikesell, Moran, Penrose, Reisman, and Tanzer fit under this broad rubric.

Barber, R. J. (1970) THE AMERICAN CORPORATION: ITS POWER, ITS MONEY, ITS POLITICS. New York: E. P. Dutton.

A former counsel for the U.S. Senate Anti-Trust Subcommittee, Richard Barber sounds the alarm about the increasing concentration in the American economy and carefully analyzes the symbiosis between business and government. Part V of the book, "The Internationalization of Business," is of particular importance. He persuasively argues that the forces of economic concentration so evident in the U.S. economy have already set in motion a trend which will produce an unprecedented degree of concentration in the world economy with serious socioeconomic and political implications.

Behrman, J. N. (1970) NATIONAL INTERESTS AND THE MULTI-NATIONAL ENTERPRISE. Englewood Cliffs, N.J.: Prentice-Hall.

While the conflict between U.S.-based multinationals and host countries in the Third World continues to attract attention and produce its share of drama and tension, relations between these corporations and the industrialized countries are by far more important, if only because the stakes involved are much larger for the parties involved. Behrman provides an insightful analysis of the sources of tension between U.S. multinationals and their more important hosts (he covers Canada, Europe, and Australia), and he explains the dynamics of what he calls the love-hate syndrome that characterizes the attitude of their governments toward the industrial giants. Need for capital, technology, and industrial development is perhaps as important as the fear of dominance, and the result is often a policy of ambivalence and confusion on the part of the host countries.

Behrman argues that the results could be catastrophic if supranational agreements and mechanisms are not developed.

Bell, D. (1971) "The Corporation and Society in the 1970's." THE PUBLIC INTEREST 24 (Summer): 5-32.

Daniel Bell argues that, in light of the urgent and pressing social problems confronting America, more attention will be focused on the corporation and, subsequently, our vision of it as an institution will become primarily social and political in nature. Unfortunately, Bell's essay and much of the debate about the social responsibility of the private corporation sweeping American social thought today are hopelessly ethnocentric. A good deal of attention is focused on the impact of the American corporation at home, but few extend the logic of their analysis to the corporate impact on a global scale. This is perhaps a testimony both to the ethnocentrism of the "corporate responsibility movement" and to the failure of most students of world society to probe the social dimensions of corporate activity.

Brown, C. C. [ed.] (1970) WORLD BUSINESS: PROMISE AND PROBLEMS. New York: Macmillan.

As in most edited books, the quality of the essays assembled here is highly uneven, and it is quite difficult to detect any unifying theme that ties the different chapters together. Most of the essays have previously appeared in the Columbia Journal of World Business and, though not interrelated, they nonetheless make a contribution.

The editor's introductory remarks express hopes about the potential contribution of the multinationals to world peace and world development that recall the ungrounded optimism of the theorists and philosophers of economic development in the early sixties. Kenneth Simmonds tests the claims of multinationality against an empirical study of the multinational corporate elite. He finds those who occupy top positions to be of the same nationality as the firms that employ them, and his findings seem to temper and cast doubt upon the rhetoric of corporate internationalism. A number of other chapters reiterate the thesis that international business is an integrative force in the world, superseding ideological differences, and contributing to the development of a peaceful and equitable world order.

Burtis, D. et al. (1972) MULTINATIONAL CORPORATION-NATION-STATE INTERACTION: AN ANNOTATED BIBLIOGRAPHY. Philadelphia: Foreign Policy Research Institute.

This is a good and thorough bibliography which adequately surveys business and trade journals, as well as a number of non-American sources. Students of international relations should find it particularly useful.

Dahl, R. A. (1970) AFTER THE REVOLUTION? AUTHORITY IN A
GOOD SOCIETY. New Haven, Conn.: Yale Univ. Press.

Though Dahl does not directly deal with multinational corporations, he
confronts the dilemmas of private corporate power that has significant
public impact but is largely unaccountable, unchecked, and unresponsive.
Dahl goes as far as exploring and proposing alternative systems of
corporate management that ought to be seriously discussed and examined.
He finds both private property and socialist solutions unacceptable and
advocates a self-management corporate system along the lines of the
Yugoslav model.

Galloway, J. F. (1971) "Multinational Enterprises as Worldwide Interest
Groups." POLITICS & SOCIETY 1 (Fall): 1-20.

Besides adequately surveying the literature on the multinationals and
presenting the contending explanations of their role in the international
system, Galloway posits several interesting propositions concerning their
impact upon world politics. He argues that multinational corporations
have enhanced the process of integration in the North Atlantic area, have
served to integrate the Third World into the world economy, and have
increased the access of the West to Communist markets. To effectively do
so, they have emerged as powerful interest groups on a global scale.
Unfortunately, Galloway fails to develop (adequately) the concept of
worldwide interest groups. How do these interest groups secure political
access and privileges in a decentralized international system, and what
channels do they use? What is their impact upon the world public interest
in the absence of competing interest groups that are as powerful and
resourceful? Does their power jeopardize the interests of other groups
(labor and underdeveloped countries, for example) who are not as
organized and as effective in their lobbying? Nonetheless, Galloway has
rendered a service, and the concept of global interest groups merits further
attention and research.

Guback, T. H. (1969) THE INTERNATIONAL FILM INDUSTRY.
Bloomington: Indiana University Press.

Guback's study reminds us that the values and policies promoted by
powerful and international firms can severely undermine the social
environment in which we live. Forces of monopoly and concentration in
the world cinema might have produced a more efficient market, but in the
process of doing so have sacrificed cultural authenticity and diversity and
have nearly destroyed the quality of cinema as an art that portrays
meaningful aspects of the human condition.

Heilbroner, R. L. (1971) "The Multinational Corporation and the Nation-State." NEW YORK REVIEW OF BOOKS (February 11): 20-25.

This essay is written in the Heilbroner tradition: it smashes pervasive myths, raises provocative questions, and advances new propositions. Heilbroner relates the growth of the multinationals to classic economic theory and argues that this phenomenal growth has already rendered obsolete our model of the international economy. The exchange of goods (upon which traditional import-export data and international economic analyses rest) must be replaced by a model based upon the internationalization of production ushered by the multinationals. Intra- and inter-company transfers and transactions are often as central to an understanding of the world economy as classic trade between two nations.

In examining the rhetoric of corporate internationalism and the grievances of economic nationalists, Heilbroner strikes a balance that illuminates both positions. He sees the conflict between corporations and nation-states as a conflict between two modes of organizing human affairs and suggests that the more powerful nations have greater freedom and latitude vis-à-vis the multinationals than the less fortunate ones in the Third World. Heilbroner, however, concludes by stating that both forms of organization are "ill-suited to the long-run development of human societies" and that alternative visions of world order might have to turn elsewhere.

Hellmann, R. (1970) THE CHALLENGE TO U.S. DOMINANCE OF THE INTERNATIONAL CORPORATION. New York: Dunellen.

A German economist, Hellmann is more optimistic about the future of Europe's economy and its ability to cope with the growth of American investiment than Servan-Schreiber. Europe, he maintains, can launch a successful counteroffensive and can invade the American market in the same way American corporations have invaded Europe. The drive toward multinationalism which took American companies to the remote corners of the world will eventually be felt by European corporations, and the American market will inevitably be a natural target. For this process to be more effective and harmonious, Hellmann recommends several sound policy proposals for those governments and corporations on both sides of the Atlantic.

Hymer, S. (1970) "The Efficiency (Contradictions) of Multinational Corporations." Economic Growth Center, Yale University. (mimeo)

Critics of multinational corporations are probably as numerous as their defenders and advocates. A brilliant economist, Stephen Hymer, shows the simplicity of adopting extreme positions. The age of the multinationals, he argues, will doubtless mean greater efficiency in the allocation of world resources, accompanied by grave social problems and inequities. This is a first-rate essay that shows both the promise and dangers of multinational corporate growth. Appropriately enough, Hymer concludes by reminding us that "the multinational corporation reveals the power of size and the danger of leaving it uncontrolled."

Jacoby, N. H. (1970) "The Multinational Corporation." CENTER MAGA-ZINE 3 (May): 37-55.

Jacoby's essay is a fine theoretical statement that explains the drive toward multinationalism as well as the impact of the multinational upon its several constituencies. As to the future of the multinational, Jacoby expresses hope and optimism and suggests that the multinational will act as an integrative force in the international system.

Jager, E. (1970) "Multinationalism and Labor: For Whose Benefit?" COLUMBIA JOURNAL OF WORLD BUSINESS 1 (January/February): 56-65.

An economist with the AFL-CIO, Elizabeth Jager provides us with an interesting analysis of how organized labor in the United States views the multinational spread of American corporations. Internationalization of production, American unions argue, weakens their position at the bargaining table, exports their jobs, and increases the flexibility and mobility of the corporation at their expense. Though the future for labor might lie in international coordination and international organization, it is doubtful that it can match and neutralize the centralization and concentration so evident in the multinational corporate structure.

Judge, A.J.N. (1968-1969) "Multinational Business Enterprises." YEAR-BOOK OF INTERNATIONAL ORGANIZATIONS. Brussells, Union of International Associations.

Realizing the importance of the multinationals, the editors of the *Yearbook of International Organizations* departed in this issue from their traditional emphasis upon nonprofit organizations and devoted some attention to the growth of multinational enterprise. Judge's study is a useful data source that develops criteria of multinationality, identifies the nationality of business firms, determines the percentage of their foreign and domestic ownership, and documents the growth of multinational business through tracing the growth of foreign corporate subsidiaries. An updating of the Judge data, which presents some slightly different findings, is presented in the 1970-1971 issue of the Yearbook by G. P. Speeckaert.

Kapp, K. W. (1971) THE SOCIAL COSTS OF PRIVATE ENTERPRISE. New York: Schocken Books.

This is a book that first appeared in 1950, long before the social costs generated by business organizations became a fashionable subject of inquiry. Kapp condemns the thrust of modern economic theory that treats social costs as externalities to be shifted to, and borne by, the society at large. Future evaluations of the performance of the economy, he argues, must account for these costs that are responsible for "increasing social disorganization, irrationality, and violence of contemporary life."

Keohane, R. O. and Nye, J. S. [eds.] (1971) INTERNATIONAL ORGANIZATION 3 (Summer).

This is a special issue of *International Organization* entitled "Transnational Relations and World Politics." The editors and the contributors, realizing the shortcomings of state-centric paradigms of world politics, bring together a number of essays that depart from the nation-state model and identify political processes that are transnational in scope and magnitude. Several articles are of particular relevance to those interested in the politics of multinational corporations. Robert Cox gives a first-rate analysis of the role of international labor in the world political system, and in the process illuminates some patterns of interaction among corporations, labor unions, and nation-states. Peter Evans refuses to accept at face value the assumption that corporations will contribute to the welfare of underdeveloped countries and gives a concise analysis of the critical perspectives on the multinationals that are prevalent in those countries. Raymond Vernon sees some dangers in the lopsided global interdependence brought about by the multinationals, and Louis Wells gives a standard description of the nature of the multinational firm.

Kindleberger, C. P. (1969) AMERICAN BUSINESS ABROAD: SIX LECTURES ON DIRECT INVESTMENT. New Haven, Conn.: Yale Univ. Press.

After providing us with a theory of direct investment and explaining the dynamics of American investment in both the developed and underdeveloped countries, Kindleberger devotes some attention to the international corporation. Much of his argument has by now become common knowledge, but this is still a valuable source for a summary of contending interpretations of the role of the international corporation in the world economy. Kindleberger too readily accepts the contention that the international corporation will serve as a force for a more egalitarian distribution of world wealth and resources.

Kindleberger, C. P. [ed.] (1970) THE INTERNATIONAL CORPORA-
TION. Cambridge, Mass.: MIT Press.

A product of a seminar that brought together an impressive number of
scholars and business practitioners, this volume presents a breadth of
perspectives and case studies of international industries and particular
countries. Two chapters merit special attention. Kenneth Waltz, a student
of world politics, challenges the notion of global interdependence and
argues that the multinationals are not eroding national sovereignty or
changing the distribution of world power. Hymer and Rowthorn demonstrate the viability of European corporations in the face of the American
challenge and suggest that the challenge is a bit exaggerated.

Kindleberger, C. P. (1970) POWER AND MONEY/THE ECONOMICS OF
INTERNATIONAL POLITICS AND THE POLITICS OF INTER-
NATIONAL ECONOMICS. New York: Basic Books.

This book is billed as an attempt to bridge the gap between
international economics and international politics. It is a sweeping
treatment of such economic and political phenomena as imperialism,
power, sovereignty, war, and corporations. With regard to corporations,
Kindleberger advances the argument that they stimulate the development
of international policies and mechanisms and "leave less room for the
independent, idiosyncratic, law-unto-itself national state." He also gives us
a basic taxonomy of corporations that distinguishes between national
firms with foreign operations, multinational firms, and, finally, international corporations.

Levitt, K. (1970) SILENT SURRENDER: THE MULTINATIONAL
CORPORATION IN CANADA. New York: St. Martin's Press.

A Canadian economist at McGill University, Levitt expresses a concern
that is shared by most Canadians: the immense power of the American
presence in the Canadian economy. To her, the prospects of economic
freedom in Canada lie in the birth of a new sense of economic nationalism,
particularly in the more strategic and vital sectors of the economy.

Levy, W. J. (1971) "Oil Power." FOREIGN AFFAIRS 4 (July): 652-668.

Walter Levy, a consultant for oil companies with significant linkages to
the industry, is hardly a neutral commentator on the problems that plague
the relation between the companies and the major producers. He contends
that oil power is basically a myth and that the balance of power has
shifted decisively in favor of the major exporters, particularly after the
creation of the Organization of Petroleum Exporting Countries (OPEC).

And what is noteworthy here is his final plea to the Western governments to restore the balance of power so that the flow of oil would be more secure and reliable.

Lieberson, S. (1971) "An Empirical Study of Military-Industrial Linkages." AMERICAN JOURNAL OF SOCIOLOGY 4 (January): 562-584.

Arguing against the theory that the American economy has become overly militarized, Lieberson fields impressive data and contends that the economy does not need significant military outlays, and he goes as far as arguing that the curtailment of military expenditures might contribute to economic growth and prosperity. Lieberson finds that military contracts are an insignificant percentage of corporate sales and concludes in favor of a pluralist interpretation of the American economy that sees military spending as one among many sets of vested and competing interests. Another sociologist, Paul Stevenson, sees little merit in Lieberson's analysis and conclusions and serious problems in the interpretation of the data. (See Paul Stevenson, "American Capitalism and Militarism: A Critique of Lieberson." AMERICAN JOURNAL OF SOCIOLOGY, July 1971: 134-138, and Lieberson's reply: 138-142.)

Magdoff, H. (1969) THE AGE OF IMPERIALISM. New York: Monthly Review Press.

In what has become a hotly contested book, Magdoff challenges the "end of imperialism" argument and attempts to explain the economic roots of America's global strategies. Contemporary imperialism, he argues, is different from its classic predecessor but no less viable in its impact upon the world economy. Corporations are seen as the vehicle of the new imperialism, pursuing policies in concert with the world's wealthy and powerful to the detriment of the majority of the world's population. An interesting debate concerning the merit of Magdoff's book took place on the pages of *Public Policy,* and it beautifully conveyed the gulf that exists between its admirers and its critics. Frank Ackerman, a graduate student at Harvard, contended that Magdoff's is the best modern statement on the economic roots of American foreign policy. Charles P. Kindleberger, on the other hand, argued that the book is "an empty collection of statistics and string of quotations" amounting to a very unimpressive effort, and that he is bewildered as to why youth find it so persuasive and appealing. (See "Magdoff on Imperialism: Two Views by Ackerman and Kindleberger," in PUBLIC POLICY, Summer 1971: 525-534.)

Melman, S. [ed.] (1971) THE WAR ECONOMY OF THE UNITED STATES. New York: St. Martin's Press.

Seymour Melman has been one of the leading proponents of disarmament and one of the leading scholars on the subject. He has investigated the impact of economic conversion, economic waste in military production, and the political dimensions of disarmament. This collection of essays deals with these and other related problems, and identifies the dangers inherent in an economy that is geared toward war and international violence.

Mikesell, R. F. [ed.] (1971) FOREIGN INVESTMENT IN THE PETROLEUM AND MINERAL INDUSTRIES: A CASE STUDY OF INVESTOR-HOST COUNTRY RELATIONS. Baltimore: Johns Hopkins Press.

Petroleum and minerals are central to the economies of many underdeveloped states. In some cases, they are virtually the only linkage between these states and the world economy, and they produce a pattern of dependence that the term "one crop" countries adequately portrays. As these primary commodities are usually produced and marketed by large international firms, the relations between these firms and the host countries acquire special significance. Mikesell brings together a number of case studies that deal with state-company relations in various extractive industries and that capture the dynamics of interaction between firms bent on maximizing their profits and maintaining their control and countries attempting to increase their revenues and to secure a level of participation in these industries.

Moran, T. H. (1971-72) "New Deal or Raw Deal in Raw Materials." FOREIGN POLICY 5 (Winter): 115-134.

This is a first-rate analysis of the confrontation between powerful and vertically integrated multinationals and economic nationalists who want a degree of control over their natural resources. Moran's sober analysis suggests that there are grave problems ahead for the nationalists, for even if they nationalize extractive industries, they must be able to secure their share of a market that is controlled by a handful of firms. Moran suggests that it is possible for the nationalists to escape one form of dependence and domination and yet find themselves living under new forms of control and dominance.

Penrose, E. (1968) THE LARGE INTERNATIONAL FIRM IN DEVELOPING COUNTRIES. Cambridge, Mass.: MIT Press.

This is an excellent study of the economics of the international oil industry by one of the leading experts on the subject. Edith Penrose provides us with an adequate explanation of the dynamics of vertical integration, a concise historical analysis of the growth of the industry, and a clear and detailed profile of the companies involved. A special section on oil in Latin America explains the problems, both unique and common, confronting Latin American countries as producers and consumers of that controversial commodity.

Perlmutter, H. V. (1969) "The Tortuous Evolution of the Multinational Corporation." COLUMBIA JOURNAL OF WORLD BUSINESS 1 (January-February): 9-18.

Perlmutter gives us a basic and sound taxonomy of corporations that distinguishes among ethnocentric, polycentric, and geocentric corporations. Ethnocentric corporations, by his definition, are oriented toward their home country, polycentric toward the host countries in which they operate, while geocentric firms respond to global needs and standards. Despite the claims, we must concur with Perlmutter that we have very few, if any, geocentric corporations. Most corporations disseminate ethnocentric norms and values and exhibit no great sensitivity toward global needs and aspirations.

Reisman, M. (1971) "Polaroid Power: Taxing Business for Human Rights." FOREIGN POLICY 5 (Fall): 101-110.

Polaroid, General Motors, and a number of other American firms have recently come under fire for their operations in South Africa. Critics argued that American corporate presence contributes to apartheid and strengthens the foundations of South Africa's economy. Reisman defends Polaroid's decision to stay in South Africa and argues that very little can be gained from withdrawal, and that withdrawal might even have a negative impact upon bringing about social change in South Africa. Economic boycotts and sanctions, he maintains, might be dramatic but they do very little to better the social conditions for South Africa's nonwhite population.

Rolfe, S. and Damm, W. (1970) THE MULTINATIONAL CORPORATION AND THE WORLD ECONOMY. New York: Praeger.

With a foreword by David Kennedy (then the U.S. Secretary of the Treasury) and a sponsorship by the Atlantic Council of the United States, the Atlantic Institute, and the Committee for Atlantic Economic Cooperation, this book expresses the opinions of influentials in business and government circles on both sides of the Atlantic. What we have here is a plea for closer and more amiable relationships between Europe and North America that would foster economic growth and interdependence. In addition, the book contains some useful data and appendices.

Sweezy, P. M. and Magdoff, H. (1969) "Notes on the Multinational Corporation." MONTHLY REVIEW 5 and 6 (October and November): 1-7 and 1-13.

As the authors tell us, this essay was prompted by the proliferation of literature on the multinationals and the notorious absence of any Marxist theorizing on the subject. Rather than filling the gap, they intended to spur Marxist theory in the direction of the multinationals. Given the polemics of business apologists and its abundance, this essay merits pariticular attention. Sweezy and Magdoff find the name "multinational corporation" both objectionable and apologetic. As all capital is nationally based, they argue that the spread of the multinational is a mere facade for the growth of American and Western capital that perpetuates, though in a slightly different way, the colonial structure of the world economy.

Tanzer, M. (1969) THE POLITICAL ECONOMY OF INTERNATIONAL OIL AND THE UNDERDEVELOPED COUNTRIES. Boston: Beacon Press.

This is a grand tour of the oil industry, by far the most political of all international industries. Tanzer's analysis is a brilliant and thorough treatment of the structure and dynamics of that industry. The particular merit of this study is its focus upon the underdeveloped importers as they seek to deal with a small number of firms that control the world market and divide it among themselves. A number of case studies of oil politics in several importing countries makes the book a unique contribution to the literature on oil.

Turner, L. (1970) INVISIBLE EMPIRES: MULTINATIONAL COMPA-NIES AND THE MODERN WORLD. London: Hamish Hamilton.

This is a thought-provoking statement by a British sociologist that is overly ambitious in what it seeks to cover. Though it lacks analytical rigor, and the empirical base for the kind of analysis it undertakes, it raises serious normative questions about the social costs of the multinationals and ventures into the area of labor's response to the flexibility of multinational firms.

Vagts, D. V. (1970) "The Multinational Enterprise: A New Challenge for Transnational Law." HARVARD LAW REVIEW 4 (February): 739-792.

A professor at the Harvard Law School, Vagts attempts to cope with the problems that the multinational enterprise poses for the international legal system. He offers some speculative models of adjustment that the legal system might develop in response to the growth of the multinational corporation and contends that the political power of the multinational is neither excessive nor formidable. And in response to those calling for international regulation, he puts forward the thought that governments may create institutions that are as remote, centalized, and inaccessible as the multinational itself.

Vaupel, J. W. and Curhan, J. P. (1969) THE MAKING OF MULTI-NATIONAL ENTERPRISE. Boston: Division of Research, Graduate School of Business Administration, Harvard University.

This is a sourcebook for data on the 187 U.S. manufacturing corporations that are the principal focus for investigation by the Harvard Project on Multinational Enterprise headed by Raymond Vernon. The volume traces the development of these large firms and their foreign subsidiaries since 1900 and serves as the basis for Vernon's major work, and forthcoming publications by scholars associated with the project. The corporations analyzed here are among the largest in the world; researchers will probably find this volume quite useful, and the data could be used to test theories and generalizations and advance hypotheses.

Vernon, R. (1971) "The Multinational Enterprise: Power Versus Sovereignty." FOREIGN AFFAIRS 4 (July): 736-751.

Much of what is stated here is more forcefully and broadly stated in the author's volume *Sovereignty at Bay*. Vernon proceeds from a basic asymmetry between multinational enterprises and national governments. He attributes this to the flexibility of the multinational firm, its ability to evade governmental power, and to the desire on the part of government to exercise economic control within its boundaries. Given the inevitable nature of this asymmetry, Vernon suggests that it might be tolerable up to a point, but some multinational methods of regulation and conflict resolution might eventually be needed.

Vernon, R. (1971) SOVEREIGNTY AT BAY: THE MULTINATIONAL SPREAD OF U.S. ENTERPRISES. New York: Basic Books.

This is the first and principal product of the Harvard Multinational Enterprise project, a large-scale, well-funded, and ambitious research effort. Forthcoming volumes will be more technical and specific, covering such aspects as financing and managing multinational enterprises, and dealing with particular industries. Vernon's study is an impressive achievement that attempts to steer an independent course in a field that is inherently explosive and controversial. Ultimately, however, the product is sympathetic to the multinationals, though sufficiently critical not to significantly load the dice in their favor.

The study is exclusively concerned with large U.S. multinationals (numbering 187) in the manufacturing and extractive industries. The structure and dynamics of these industries and of the corporations involved receive a superb analysis that is thorough and documented. It is quite difficult to match the analysis here, if only because of the collective effort behind it. The impact of the multinationals upon national economies and national ideologies is also explored. While in the last analysis some might disagree with Vernon's orientation, and inevitably so, this is perhaps the most authoritative statement on the subject and will probably serve as a point of departure—to agree with or to refute—for several years to come.

Wilkins, M. (1970) THE EMERGENCE OF MULTINATIONAL ENTER-PRISE. Cambridge, Mass.: Harvard Univ. Press.

Mira Wilkins traces the drive toward internationalization on the part of American corporations up to 1914. A second volume (date of publication still unknown) will bring the research to the present. The first volume provides us with adequate insight into the history and organizational logic of overseas expansion on the part of American business. It is weakened, however, by Wilkins' completely apolitical model of this international growth. Time and again she dismisses the political dimensions of this growth and maintains that American firms expanded into overseas markets independently of the policies of the U.S. government.